A-Z

of Emotional Abuse

Elizabeth Goddard

This edition is published by Revive Your Soul Publishing in 2019

www.reviveyoursoul.com

Elizabeth has the unique ability to combine wisdom from the heart with wisdom from the mind. She is sharing deep insights into patterns of abusive relationships. I love how she has put those into the A to Z categories, this gives this book both, a good read plus also a reference tool. I know Elizabeth personally, and she is such a heart-warming person, living from joy and you can feel she has come a long way. She knows what she is talking about. I can highly recommend her books.

Caroline Palmy • Author, Speaker and Healer

A-Z of Emotional Abuse by Elizabeth Goddard is a very thought provoking book to read. It gives a very simple, clear description of what it is like being in an emotionally abusive relationship. This book is a great tool to share with someone that you may think is being emotionally abused. It will help them understand the stages of the abuse and what happens in those stages. It is very easy to read and keeps you focused on the content.

Dana Zimmerman • Author

Part of healing from trauma is learning to trust yourself again. You cannot learn to trust yourself again unless you understand how you were deceived...until you understand the process by which your abuser divorced you from yourself. Liz's book is healing because it does just that...helps you see where are, so you can figure out where you are going.

Cathryn Abbott Jones • Author

Books by Elizabeth Goddard

Finding Lily

For information about Elizabeth Goddard's courses and coaching support please visit her website

reviveyoursoul.co.uk

Contents

The Hopi Creation Story

The Creator gathered all of Creation and said, "I want to hide something from humans until they are ready for it. It's the realisation that they create their own reality".

The Eagle said, "Give it to me. I will take it to the moon".

The Creator said, "No. One day they will go there and find it".

The Salmon said, "I will bury it on the bottom of the ocean".

The Creator said, "No. One day they will go there too".

The Buffalo said, "I will bury it on the Great Plains".

The Creator said, "They will cut into the skin of the Earth and find it even there".

Grandmother Mole who lives in the breast of Mother Earth, and who has no physical eyes but sees with spiritual eyes said,

"Put it inside of them".

And the Creator said, "It is done".

I dedicate this book to everyone who has touched my life in some way, intentionally or unintentionally, that has allowed me to heal and grow.

To my children, whom I have managed to "fuck up" and have taught me so much, I can only hope they can eventually forgive me on some level.

I dedicate this book to you for picking it up and flicking through the pages, wanting to heal the wounds and knowing now is the time.

Acknowledgements

My heart explodes with gratitude for the help and support I received writing this book.

To Alison, Angela, Janet and Karen who supported me in various ways through the journey of writing this book.

To the people who have walked into my life and given me the experiences which have allowed me to Crack Open and allow the light to shine in. Each one I have experienced as a Dark Night of the Soul, but has made me stronger.

And to Sean for having the idea of turning my Instagram posts into a book, I am deeply grateful for his insight and vision.

Is it time?

Like a diamond we are all multi-faceted, we have so many different faces and elements to our personalities. Step outside yourself, watch how you behave with different people.

If you have friends from your childhood as an adult you may all revert to a slightly less mature behaviour, and when you are at work you might behave differently with colleagues than you do with your boss.

Each of us possesses a uniqueness within. It is a sacred place inside us: in the Hopi Indian Story at the beginning the Creator wants to hide something until we are ready and it is put inside us.

To desire change, you need to go inside, explore your internal universe and reclaim the hidden treasures.

I was listening to Debbie Ford's book *The Dark Side of the Light Chasers*[1,] in it is she used John Welwood's analogy *The Castle*[2]. He described us as castles: full of rooms and corridors, basements and attics; each room representing a part of us that contains a unique gift.

He said that as a child "we explored our rooms without SHAME or judgement". As people visited our castle they may have told us they didn't like something so we closed the door to that room and to that part of ourselves.

Think of the people who have walked in and out of your life. With each relationship, different people gave you their views of what you should be like or what they liked or didn't like about you.

I can relate to this in my career, if I wanted to get promoted I was told I needed to conform or behave in a certain way.

And this has also been true in relationships, particularly EMOTIONALLY ABUSIVE ones where CONDITIONAL LOVE was being expressed.

This is where we have to be really careful as parents and caregivers, not repeating the pattern or the learnt behaviour.

So gradually over time you closed door after door and Debbie Ford[1] describes it as "one day waking up and being a two bed semi".

Perhaps you were told your rooms were too loud, or the colours were too bright, or maybe your rooms were too quiet or the colours clashed. You might have realised you had rooms that no one else had, so you closed them off to the public not knowing what to do with them.

John Welwood[2] said "We can only find the key to our uniqueness by opening all the rooms in our castle.".

Which might be quite scary and daunting or it might appeal to you and be exciting... Think of it like taking off the dust sheets uncovering the rooms of love and courage of elegance and grace, you may still have part of the rooms open, but just protect a few elements in there. Opening up the rooms of creativity and femininity, honesty and integrity; of health, assertiveness, sexiness and power. Throwing open the doors and windows to the rooms of timidity and hatred, greed and frigidity; and the rooms of laziness, arrogance, sickness, and evil, shining the light in them and exploring them.

The conditioning that comes from our childhood makes us scared of what we might find lurking behind the doors, many of which are dusty or the locks are rusty. Rather than setting off on the adventure of self-discovery, we pretend they never existed.

Your castle was full of light, love, and wonder.

Is this now your time?

Embrace each and every facet!

Shine bright like a diamond!

In the Beginning

I remember it like it was yesterday, there are so many things I can't remember but this memory is so clear.

I was sitting on the arm of my sofa holding a coffee; the October sun streaming through the large window, and then it happened; I made this huge statement "I don't ever want anyone to go through what I have been through".

BOOM

And there it was...

The words were out of my mouth and they couldn't be unsaid or unheard.

A thousand horses could not drag them back.

The Seed was planted!

At this point I had no idea what I was going to go through, it was just terribly painful; and I had no idea that I was in fact at the start of my journey, not the end as I thought...

I still believed this was all my fault.

It wasn't until months later I realised I actually didn't want to stop people going through their own personal journey and I didn't want them having their own cathartic Dark Night of the Soul, because this is where the magic is... This is where the healing happens.

What I did want was to help people recover, and hopefully a lot quicker than I did. And I could help them find the information they would need to understand what happened because I believe KNOWLEDGE is POWER.

I started off by asking "what happened?" which was usually followed by "who does that". As I fell down in to a dark hole of FEAR and total despair, there was a pain emanating deep within my Soul and I replayed the relationship asking the QUESTIONS "what if?" and "maybe..." believing that if I had done something or said something differently I wouldn't be here.

Of course this was a lie, it was the TRAUMA BONDING that was keeping me trapped.

I have been so grateful for the chance to heal; I had been broken open and those cracks allowed the light to shine in.

I knew for me it was going to be a long slow process because I wanted to understand each stage. And I knew I was going to have to face many shadow parts I didn't like about myself: parts I shielded from the world.

Just like an egg: "If an egg is broken by an outside force, life ends. If broken by an inside force, life begins. Great things always begin from the inside." Real change can only come from within.

Unknown

Through my own healing journey, I know the damage EMOTIONAL ABUSE leaves in your life, physically, mentally, emotionally and spiritually.

This was a game and I didn't have the rules. I was a shell of my former self and I'd lost everything; I was broke, and I was broken...

And I was stuck in a debilitating cycle of QUESTIONING and doubting myself - "If only I had said... If only I hadn't said... Maybe if I had done... Maybe if I hadn't done..."

I believed it was all my fault.

The very first part of healing was dealing with TRAUMA BONDING. I then realised the outcome really wouldn't have changed if I had said or done anything differently, and that CLOSURE wasn't something I was going to get.

I believe the emotions we feel are trapped trauma, we experience them over and over again until we remove them completely from our bodies.

We need to get to the core of these issues, to the root cause; and, much like a verruca, if a tiny part of the root is left it will lie dormant until it is TRIGGERED again.

The problem with a lot of methods is that they only scratch the surface of the problem and act more like a band-aid rather than a full solution...

Every step I had taken over the last twenty years had brought me to this point; each new level of understanding has expanded my toolbox.

At the heart of the work I do is a deep healing technique (identifying the root cause and removing it) and powerful life-changing processes for healing.

And helping people to reclaim their power or, in a lot of cases, reclaim themselves feeling whole again for the very first time.

Elizabeth

Author and Emotional Abuse Coach

Credit: Photo by Volkan Olmez on Unsplash

There is complete silence around her, but I can feel her heart breaking. It is being cracked open and I can hear a silent sobbing coming from deep inside her, but for an outsider, you wouldn't know that, you can't hear it.

• Elizabeth Goddard • Finding Lily •

Introduction

You might be in the throes of confusion; either at the end or nearly at the end, of an EMOTIONALLY ABUSIVE or TOXIC Relationship.

Or perhaps this happened to you years ago and you still haven't recovered from it, dragging the emotional trauma from relationship to relationship...

Why are these types of relationships so hard to heal from?

The damage caused puts you into a state of confusion, you had no idea that the ABUSE was taking place; like Chinese water torture, it happened very, very slowly and it turned you insane!

What if this happened for a reason?

There is something magical about you, something pure; your energy, your creativity, your laughter. There was something very unique about you that was needed by your ABUSER and you were picked and groomed!

Everything you said and did was watched and noted. The interest in you was not exactly what you thought it was.

You were swept off your feet with compliments, gifts, days out, meals out; your every need was catered for (if this happened on a lesser scale, I will address this separately). You may have woken in the morning to find a message from them; this was deliberate, ensuring they were the first thing you thought about.

And perhaps they did the same at the end of the day; sweet dreams...

I, like many people, have been hurt by a TOXIC, or an EMOTIONALLY ABUSIVE, person, and in my case, it was not just one, I've managed to notch up a few...

There is a wounding to the Soul you don't believe you will ever recover from.

To Label or not to Label

The definition of label is 1. a small piece of paper, fabric, plastic, or similar material attached to an OBJECT and giving information about it. 2. a classifying phrase or name applied to a person or thing, especially one that is inaccurate or restrictive.

If you find it helpful, use a label; if it helps you identify with something, especially if it will be beneficial to your healing.

When I started on this part of my healing journey I couldn't identify as a CO-DEPENDANT. It didn't sit well; it was like wearing an itchy jumper. I listened to Ross Rosenburg's book *The Human Magnet Syndrome*[3] and he spoke about the dance between the NARCISSIST and the CO-DEPENDANT and it made me squirm. However, I was able to identify with the label EMPATH and I used that until I was able to heal my CO-DEPENDANT side.

There is a reason these relationships are so comfortable and why they feel so familiar, that intense connection and the powerful attraction.

You may find it helpful to use a label; you might not. It might help you to understand the emotions and the trauma you are experiencing, but it might not.

This is your journey and only you will know what feels right or what feels right for you at this time.

Start to listen to your body and understand what it needs.

The Narcissist, the Sociopath and the Psychopath.

I try not to use the labels of NARCISSIST, SOCIOPATH or PSYCHOPATH in this book, but they do appear.

Firstly, these personality types cannot take RESPONSIBILITY for the untold damage they cause, in fact they walk away, playing the VICTIM.

Secondly, the diagnosis for a personality disorder is given by a mental health professional and, because they don't see anything wrong with them or their behaviour, they are not going to seek help.

Perhaps you are trying to understand what happened and wondering why you are feeling like this, maybe you are discovering this new information and you are asking yourself if you are the NARCISSIST, this is so common!

Am I a Narcissist?

The fact that you are asking that QUESTION should hopefully put your mind at rest: they can't take RESPONSIBILITY so it isn't something the ABUSER would ask.

We are all on the scale, in fact we are all on every scale.

As a baby you were naturally self-centred you needed to be for your survival. You alerted your parents or caregiver to tend to your needs by crying. Over time this changed, as you grew, you were shown how to manage your feelings and your needs.

If you have spent any significant amount of time with a NARCISSIST, you may have picked up a few traits - you may have been asking; "Who does that to another person?" or "Why does it hurt so much?" "Do I have EMPATHY?" or "Am I a NARCISSIST?" These are not QUESTIONS someone with a personality disorder would ever consider.

You could be wondering if you are a NARCISSIST because you have been told this is your fault. During the DEVALUATION and DISCARD stages, they have told you what is wrong with you and why the relationship is breaking down, and you did whatever you could to fix it - losing more and more of yourself.

Or it could be that you grew up with one or more NARCISSISTIC people in your life and you have picked up some of their traits (see below CHILDREN ARE SPONGES and NARCISSISTIC FLEAS).

This does not make you a NARCISSIST.

We are all on the spectrum.

The Original Wound

Believe me when I say I understand what you have experienced is horrific.

Each story is different, but the pattern is the same; IDEALISATION, DEVALUATION and DISCARD, and this cycle can go on for years.

The longer it goes on - the more ENMESHED you become, the invisible chains trapping you.

But what if there was a way of turning this grit into gold?

There may be a few childhood wounds and I believe these are the reasons you have experienced this relationship. I lost track of how many 3-year-olds, 5-year-olds and 8-year-olds that I needed to heal.

Much like a verruca, which is a virus that penetrates all the levels of the skin, if the full root isn't removed it lays dormant until it is TRIGGERED again. And this is the same for The ORIGINAL WOUND: if you do not fully heal the wound, it will appear again, you will keep meeting people who treat you the same way.

It causes so much damage...

Long-term contact with a TOXIC or EMOTIONALLY ABUSIVE person causes damage to the brain.

ABUSE causes damage to the Hippocampus, which is a structure found on either side of the brain that is in the shape of a seahorse. This is the area we use for learning and memory.

Damage to the Hippocampus can result in memory loss.

The stress caused by an EMOTIONALLY ABUSIVE relationship TRIGGERS the hormones cortisol, adrenaline and noradrenaline, which causes the Hippocampus to shrink.

This can happen when a child or adult is under constant threat from intimidating or bullying behaviour. This could be the FEAR of ABANDONMENT or the destruction of a favourite toy or OBJECT.

The damage to the Hippocampus can happen when a child or adult experiences criticism, BELITTLING, name-calling, yelling, swearing or verbal humiliation.

It can occur when children and adults are ISOLATED from friends and family, not allowing them to have friends or preventing them from attending groups or classes outside the home.

Research[4] from Yale and Stanford University using veterans and VICTIMS of childhood ABUSE (suffering from post-traumatic stress disorder) used MRI scans to show the reduction in the Hippocampus. These studies showed that traumatic or highly stressful experiences can have long-term effects on the structure and function of the brain.

When we experience stress, our body receives the hormone cortisol causing the FIGHT or FLIGHT response. And high levels of cortisol may damage cells in the Hippocampus.

We are all a Bunch of Chemicals!

We are all a bunch of chemicals all held together in our skin. If you think back to school and your science lessons, when chemicals were mixed together, there was a reaction: we are the same. You may have experienced this when you have met someone for the first time, and it caused a reaction within you; there is may have been an instant attraction or an instant dislike, these are chemical reactions within your body.

When you experience trauma, your stress hormones are TRIGGERED, there is a chemical reaction within your body (see the FOUR F's).

When you are in, or recovering from, an EMOTIONALLY ABUSIVE or TOXIC relationship, the way you are feeling could be due to the chemicals RAGING around your body. Think of a teenager who can't communicate, and their emotions are everywhere, you are not quite sure when they open their mouths who you are going to get... Does this sound familiar?

When I started my journey, a lot of people were talking about the addiction to DOPAMINE; but my interest was in the role that OXYTOCIN plays in these relationships as well. It is the BONDING hormone that helps us create trust.

Dr Helen Fisher[5] and her team at Rutgers University discovered romantic love can be broken down into three categories: **Lust, Attraction**, and **Attachment**.

Lust: Testosterone and Oestrogen

Attraction: DOPAMINE, Norepinephrine and Serotonin

Attachment: OXYTOCIN and Vasopressin

Lust is driven by the desire for sexual gratification.

The hypothalamus plays a role in this, stimulating the production of the sex hormones Oestrogen and Testosterone and men and women have both.

We can lust after someone we are attracted to, and a person can lust after another without it being reciprocated.

Attraction involves the pathways in the brain that CONTROL the "reward" behaviour. DOPAMINE, which is produced by the hypothalamus, is released when we do things that feel good to us.

DOPAMINE and Norepinephrine are released when we are attracted to someone, and can make us feel giddy with excitement, or we may feel more energetic, and it can even lead to a decreased appetite and insomnia. Norepinephrine, also known as noradrenaline, plays a large role in the FIGHT or FLIGHT response (see The FOUR F's).

The attraction seems to lead to a reduction in serotonin, a hormone that's known to be involved in appetite and mood.

Attachment is the dominant factor in long-term relationships, and this is why my interest is so high in this chemical.

Lust and Attraction are mainly found in romantic entanglements, the attachment is needed to BOND friendships. It is needed for parent-infant BONDING or any relationship where trust is needed (see OXYTOCIN).

DOPAMINE is the hormone RESPONSIBLE for the brain's reward centre. And a lot of research has been carried out on the DOPAMINE pathway and addiction.

The same regions that light up when we are attracted to someone, light up when a person takes cocaine. Cocaine maintains the DOPAMINE signalling for much longer. And the same brain regions also light up when we become addicted to material goods as well as when we become emotionally dependent on our partners.

You may hear people describe the emotions at the end of an EMOTIONALLY ABUSIVE relationship are like an addict going through withdrawal.

Too much DOPAMINE in a relationship can underlie unhealthy emotional dependence on our partners.

And it is the same with OXYTOCIN, they say too much of a good thing can actually be bad for you and it is true.

Studies on drugs such as MDMA and GHB shows that OXYTOCIN may be the hormone behind the feel-good, sociable effects these chemicals produce, causing the user to dissociate from their environment and act out of character, even recklessly.

OXYTOCIN works as a BONDING hormone, reinforcing the positive feelings we feel towards the people we love, reminding us why we like these people and increasing our affection for them.

This was a MANUFACTURED relationship, the BONDING that took place was different from a normal healthy relationship. And because of this, it moved too quickly through the stages of lust and attraction, you may have seen the RED FLAGS, but you were giddy with the chemical rushes.

Research[7] has discovered that OXYTOCIN is in fact two-faced and is RESPONSIBLE for strengthening a stressful situation, experiencing TRIGGERS of FEAR and anxiety (see OXYTOCIN).

The FOUR F's

FIGHT FLIGHT FAWN FREEZE

You may have heard of FIGHT and FLIGHT, I had, but it wasn't until a few years ago that I discovered FAWN and FREEZE.

FIGHT and FLIGHT are stress responses when faced with a dangerous situation, we make an instant decision - we either stay and FIGHT, or run (take FLIGHT). Our brains make a split decision by scanning the area and deciding if we can get away safely or if we need to stay and FIGHT and adrenaline is released into the body.

FAWNING is a response used when a person perceives a threat, instead of running away or fighting they respond in a pleasing way.

This technique is used to try to calm down and stall the threat of the attacker, talking their way out of a situation or displaying exaggerated flattery or affection towards the ABUSER.

FREEZE is the response TRIGGERED when a person can't win; they can't FIGHT or take FLIGHT and they can't calm down the situation.

Animals use FREEZE by playing dead, and my experience of FREEZE was feeling my chin tilt to the left and I was paralysed temporarily, my body froze, but my brain was still working, trying to understand what was happening and why I couldn't move.

Stress can be healthy, it keeps us focused and alert, but when it is experienced over a long period of time is very harmful (see We are all a Bunch of Chemicals!).

Children are Sponges

Children are sponges, and between birth to around seven or eight, we live in a Theta State, which is a hypnotic state, everything we see and hear, we believe to be true. It isn't until we are older and start visiting other people's homes, that we realise they do things differently. My brother describes it as the different smell - when you walk in a home and it isn't the same as yours.

The words children hear and what they witness become ingrained into their subconscious mind; the messages they receive tell them what is acceptable behaviour and what isn't.

As children, we take on the beliefs of the adults in our lives. It might be that you come from a long line of doctors or lawyers, and the expectation is you will follow them.

I have lost track of the people I've met who went into a career to please a parent.

If you have young children, and you believe you are in an ABUSIVE relationship, what are you teaching them?

Do you want your daughter or son to experience the emotions you are feeling?

The A-Z of EMOTIONAL ABUSE describes some of the words you will hear as you enter this new place of learning and healing.

It describes the techniques that were used to MANIPULATE you.

If you are experiencing really powerful traumatic reactions to anything, please seek medical help.

This book has been written in past and present tense. I use past tense for the behaviour when you were in the relationship and present tense for being out of the relationship; if you are still in the relationship please feel free to change it.

When you see words in CAPITAL LETTERS you will find a reference to it the A-Z.

I Believe Knowledge is Power!

Disclaimer

I am a thriver, I am not a victim or a survivor, this experience changed my life for the better.

I have read and studied a great deal in this area, but by no means exhaustively.

I offer my insights and advice for guidance only.

In the beginning, there was only Chaos, the gaping emptiness. Then, either all by themselves, or out of the formless void, sprang forth three more primordial deities: Gaea (Earth), Tartarus (the Underworld), and Eros (Love). Once Love was there, Gaea and Chaos – two female deities – were able to procreate and shape everything known and unknown in the Universe.

greekmythology.com

In the beginning...

In the beginning of the relationship the EMOTIONAL ABUSER listened and MIRRORED what was important to you, they then repeated everything back as if these were their own ideas, hopes and dreams.

They then put on a MASK and played the character they believed you were looking for and they did this superbly.

This is actually a sad story for everyone, but it doesn't make their behaviour right or excusable.

It is sad for the damage they did to you and sad for them. They are so empty inside; they were trying to fill the void by pretending to be someone else.

Their behaviour is despicable, what they do and how they treat people is dishonourable - however, can you imagine feeling that hollow?

Perhaps you can, maybe this is what you are feeling at the moment.

Empty and LONELY, despising every part of your being. It feels awful, I know I have been there...

But the good news is, you can heal and move on, they won't!

This was never their fault...

Something stops the ABUSER from taking RESPONSIBILITY for their actions. They will just move on to the next person, taking what they learned from you and more honed and refined techniques.

I believe that a severely damaged inner child is at the root of this. If you think back carefully, they will have exposed that child on many occasions. They may have confided in you about their awful childhood, always playing the VICTIM, but they will also have showed you the age they were damaged, by the way they behaved in certain situations. If you think back do you remember how they reacted or they may have taken on the physical behaviour of a child.

During the initial stage of your relationship, they begin not only to take over your life but also your future. They created a BOND that later became so hard for you to let go of.

The Fake Future.

You may be now realising nothing about your relationship was real.

However, the stories were so believable, you took part in the planning of them, but perhaps your dreams were completely forgotten, or they were ENMESHED into the MANUFACTURED future you were creating together.

And you go from believing you were the centre of their universe to your ABUSER turning their back on you, leaving you wondering "what the hell happened".

You weren't to know this was a game.

You had so much to give, and like a vampire, they sucked the life out of you.

Perhaps they told you that you shared the same insecurities, and you probably did, really, they were a MIRROR into your Soul.

For you, this was part of the gift to show you where you needed healing; for them, however, this was really a stage to perform.

They love to play the VICTIM; did you hear about their awful childhood? The way they were treated by their parents or a parent, the way they were treated by an employer or an ex-partner?

You listened to their stories and were praised for this, and they raised you higher on the pedestal. You were told that no one has ever understood them as you do. They compared you to their exes and you wanted to do more and more for them, to show how much you cared.

Perhaps you had never experienced this much attention before or had anyone so interested in you and what you had to say. During this time, you were also told the stories of why their relationships didn't last, and on some level, you vowed to yourself that you weren't going to make that mistake...

They targeted you, they knew you would do anything to help them, they did their research and tested your behaviour to see how far you would go, how much of yourself you were prepared to give up.

And because of this, you didn't QUESTION what the common denominator is in their relationships...

Perhaps they repeatedly told you "We are meant to be together. We are SOULMATES!" They love the idea of being a romantic; they love the attention they get from it. They were creating an invisible BOND; the more they talk about it, the more you started to believe them...

Think about it; you had so much in common, you were starting to map out your FAKE FUTURE together! They were the person of your dreams. You were beautiful and you were the only person (so far) that had really understood who they were and their needs. OF COURSE, YOU WERE SOULMATES!

And the Oscar goes to....

And you were HOOKED - it was that simple (for them).

I believe this was a gift, given to you by the Universe to heal a WOUND or many WOUNDS from your childhood. You may not agree at the moment, the pain you are feeling is still raw and painful, but I hope in time you will see it.

And I hope you will take this opportunity to heal those wounds.

You will eventually look back and realise how far you have come.

You are an amazing person!

I know you are hurting and have been for a long time, but NOW is the time to fall back in LOVE with you!

Short Relationships

For a shorter relationship, you may have experienced the same intensity. You may not have received as many gifts or meals out, but there were promises of them which never materialised.

There was the FAKE FUTURE, the comparison to the exes, how amazing you were... However very quickly you found you were at the DISCARD stage, probably skipping DEVALUATION. They GHOSTED you, and you were left wondering what happened.

It was very possible you were filling a gap whilst the ABUSER was lining up their next main SOURCE OF SUPPLY or ensuring they were secured in place. Or they might have been bored at home and in need of additional attention.

You are so special - they were right there!

They said it for a different reason, one that served them.

And just because this was a short relationship doesn't mean it is any less painful, it is as painful as being a permanent SOURCE OF SUPPLY.

Triggers and #metoo

During the #metoo movement a lot of men were affected by the stories being told. Not because they were being accused of ABUSE, but because they saw the inappropriate behaviour and hadn't done anything about it. They were moved emotionally, I saw some crying listening to what it had been like for women to experience this ABUSE. #metoo was originally used by *Tarana Burke*[6] promoting empowerment through EMPATHY for women of colour who had been sexually ABUSED.

The term exploded On October 15, 2017, American actress Alyssa Milano posted on Twitter, *"If all the women who have ever been sexually harassed or assaulted wrote "Me too." as a status, then we give people a sense of the magnitude of the problem,"* saying that she got the idea from a friend following accusations. This was following the allegations of the behaviour of Harvey Weinstein had been released in the press.

These men were being TRIGGERED by the stories, their emotions were activated by this behaviour or the stories, some said they had witnessed the behaviour and turned a blind eye to it.

If you are reading this for someone else and being TRIGGERED, please speak to someone or seek help to manage these emotions.

You might have seen this behaviour in your family, a sibling might have been the SCAPEGOAT and you are now beginning to understand what they experienced.

You might have seen a colleague be the target of this behaviour and are now recognising it.

If you are now consumed with guilt at not speaking up or standing up for someone, or challenging the behaviour please speak to someone who is experienced in this area; you may find the Ho'oponopono[28] exercise at the end of the book helpful.

I worked with one client whose siblings were allowed to torment her, copying the behaviour of their parents. Another client was regularly triangulated along with her siblings, creating competition between them all. I have worked with a few women whose mothers needed to be in CONTROL and took over their daughters' relationships, dictating who they could and couldn't be friends with and when they married put themselves in the middle of the marriage.

I worked with a client who studied and trained for years to become the top of her profession and was targeted in the office by a junior colleague. She asked for help from her manager and her colleagues, who either didn't see there was a problem or notice the behaviour or turned their backs on her. She left for a lower position with another company and was contacted by some months later and informed the colleague had turned their attention to someone else in the company.

I have worked with women who have been bullied in the workplace and overlooked for promotion because they spoke out about bad behaviour.

And I have witnessed certain behaviour and wished afterwards I had done more to help or protect someone else, but I wasn't able to at the time. I have had to forgive myself for that.

Finally, for anyone reading this for a friend or family member you believe is going through this, please don't judge them, they will do that themselves. Thankfully you will never experience what they are going through or have been through.

People do not speak about this because they are too embarrassed or feel stupid for allowing this to happen.

Offer UNCONDITIONAL LOVE and make sure they know you are there, no judgement and help them find a group or a tribe of people who have been through a similar experience. If you have never experienced this type of ABUSE you are not able to understand the depths this goes to, and the trauma it causes to the body, mind and Soul.

A-Z

of Emotional Abuse

Elizabeth Goddard

A
is for...
reviveyoursoul.co.uk

When pain knocks at the door - wise ones breathe deep and say: "Come in. Sit down with me. And don't leave until you've taught me what I need to know".

Glennon Doyle • Momastery

A is for

A is for ABANDONMENT • The definition of ABANDONMENT is the action or fact of abandoning or being abandoned. People get ABANDONED, houses get ABANDONED, villages get ABANDONED.

The emotional pain you are experiencing from being ABANDONED is from a WOUND you were given in childhood. This pain emanates deep within you.

It is a mixture or a swirling mass of emotions which include LONELINESS, LOW SELF-ESTEEM, untruths and withdrawal symptoms (see We are all a bunch of chemicals!).

The ABUSER'S greatest FEAR is being ABANDONED and they used various techniques to BOND you in the relationship, securing you as a good source of SUPPLY to them. Then, when they have finished feeding from you, they have sucked the Soul out of you like a DEMENTOR, they ABANDON you.

You are left wondering 'What happened?' You did everything you were asked to do and more, and you are left desperate for the highs you received, a shell of your former self, nothing left and not knowing how to function, or who you even are.

A is for ABUSE • The definition of ABUSE is to use something to bad effect or for a bad purpose, perhaps this is the ABUSE of alcohol and drugs. It is to treat a person or animal with cruelty or violence. A person in authority can ABUSE their power. Abuse is to assault someone or treat them in such a way as to cause damage or harm. Or to speak to someone in an insulting and offensive way. (see COERCIVE CONTROL).

A is for ABUSIVE CYCLES • The ongoing rotation of destructive behaviour used to gain POWER and CONTROL over a person. The CYCLE OF ABUSE is IDEALISATION • DEVALUATION • DISCARD.

In the beginning, there was chaos... I went to write a blog post and put in the search bar [in the beginning] thinking it would give me some information on Genesis 1:1 and the creation of heaven and earth; instead I was reading about chaos and the gaping emptiness...

Perhaps you experienced the chaos and the emptiness, or you may still be experiencing it, at the end of the relationship.

Believe me, if you heal these wounds, this will be the best gift you will ever receive.

Out of this chaos comes a love.

A love you will never have experienced before in your life. Not the MANUFACTURED love.

The CYCLE OF ABUSE is everything. It is the beginning and it is the end.

That pain deep within your Soul, screaming to be heard, is guiding you to look at the wounds and advising you that now is the time to look at them and heal them.

The CYCLE OF ABUSE is made up of three elements, IDEALISATION, DEVALUATION and DISCARD. And each element is carried out with precision for the desired results.

The chaos is the destruction left at the end of the relationship; the ABUSER walks away without a backward glance, having secured in place their next source of SUPPLY.

You may be at this point trying to understand what happened, you may be trying to label the ABUSER.

Your head may be swimming with all the information now out in the big wide web.

Your ABUSER is so empty inside. Once they have sucked out of your Soul, they leave.

You very possibly experienced IDEALISATION, where you were the centre of their world. They told you how amazing you were and showered you with gifts and meals and days out.

Over a period of time, this changed. Suddenly the things they loved about you were turned against you. The words of IDEALISATION became criticism and put-downs.

This was followed by the DISCARD, temporary at first, they always came back with the attention you were used to. You sighed with relief, and you may have vowed to yourself you wouldn't let that happen again.

This was a game; you didn't have the rules...

There were invisible chains that held you in place, it is now time to dissolve them and to repair the damage and to find out where The ORIGINAL WOUND comes from.

This is the start of a beautiful journey!

A is for ADRENAL FATIGUE • The adrenals are glands that sit on top of the kidneys which produce hormones. One of the important hormones produced here is Cortisol. Cortisol helps with our response to stress. FATIGUE is a term used to describe an overall feeling of tiredness or lack of energy, but unlike feeling sleepy or tired, FATIGUE is having no energy from the moment you wake until the moment you go to bed and on a loop, day after day after day.

ADRENAL FATIGUE is a term used to describe non-specific symptoms. The term is not recognised by health professionals but alternative health practitioners have more of an understanding. The term was coined at the end of the 1990s by *James Wilson*[8] a naturopath and chiropractor.

The Hypothalamus (which is a small region of the brain, located near the pituitary gland) perceives stress. It sends a message to the pituitary gland, which then sends a message to your ADRENALS to release hormones for FIGHT or FLIGHT. As I describe in THE FOUR F's this response is designed to be short-term, and then the body goes into recovery.

But when there is a continuous release of these hormones our bodies never get a chance to recover, putting so much pressure not only on the body but on the ADRENAL glands causing an imbalance in cortisol. You wake up tired, perhaps sleeping through your alarm or hitting the snooze button. You may find your energy crashing during the day and during the evening you may fall asleep and when you go to bed you are wide awake for hours. (see C-PTSD) C-PTSD is the result of being subjected to Traumatic situations on a regular basis with no respite.

Create space in your life. Go outside whenever possible, if you can, go barefoot. Try going barefoot around your home.

Find places that you feel safe and that make you feel calm.

Make sure you breathe consciously during the day; long deep breaths that help calm your nervous system. Try counting your breaths in and out and this also briefly quietens the mind. Breathe in counting to 8 and then hold for 8 and then breathe out for a count of 12.

Run a bath and light a candle and try relaxing, you might find to start with you can only lie there for a few minutes but over time this will get longer.

A is for ALIENATION • This tool was used to sabotage your relationships which resulted in you being cut off from your friends and family. You might have found you were no longer attending a group or club and you no longer had a support network.

The EMOTIONAL ABUSER or TOXIC person may have made up stories about the people in your life; feeding you information making you QUESTION those relationships and making you wonder if you could trust these people. By using the tactic of ALIENATION what they were really doing was wanting you to hand over your Power and take over CONTROL of your life. They wanted you to believe they were the only person who you should trust.

In families, it might have been a parent who influenced the relationship their child had with the other parent or siblings (see SCAPEGOAT and GOLDEN CHILD), or they influence the relationships the child had with friends or romantic relationships. The parent wants to maintain CONTROL over their child's life.

An EMOTIONALLY ABUSIVE or TOXIC parent can't see where they end and their child begins. It is as if the umbilical cord wasn't cut at birth, they want to be the one their child turns to for support and advice. They may be highly critical of friends their child makes or even want to CONTROL those relationships.

In romantic relationships, you were ALIENATED as the ABUSER couldn't risk you speaking to anyone who may have exposed who they really are.

You may have wanted to help them heal. They spent hours telling you about their awful childhood, perhaps you wanted to help them heal their damaged inner child. This is particularly true if you are an EMPATH, as EMPATHS are their favourite snack.

A is for ANGER • see NARCISSISTIC RAGE

A is for AVOIDANCE • AVOIDANCE is a tactic used for withdrawing from a relationship or situation. It reduces the risk of being rejected or held accountable, it is also used to avoid criticism and to stop the ABUSER from being exposed.

We all have access to this behaviour, like many that are in this list. Have you ever been confronted with a situation that you were not comfortable with, it might have been talking to a group of people or going to the dentist. You may have tried to find reasons not to attend, but you were aware of why you needed to.

When AVOIDANCE is used in a dysfunctional way, it is to take CONTROL of another person's life.

This behaviour was designed to make you feel frustrated or confused, you may have found yourself being forced to choose between the EMOTIONAL ABUSER and your friends and family.

B
is for...
reviveyoursoul.co.uk

In the end, only three things matter: how much you loved, how gently you lived, and how gracefully you let go of things not meant for you.

Buddha

B is for

B is for BAITING • BAITING is used to gain an emotional response from a person, usually in the form of an angry, aggressive or emotional reaction.

The normally easy going you may have found yourself experiencing emotions foreign to you.

When animals are used for BAITING, they are worried or tormented, being pitted against each other, usually for the purpose of entertainment.

It is the same in personal relationships.

This was done for POWER and CONTROL, a way of deflecting their own behaviour, or the attention away from them.

During the IDEALISATION stage they encouraged you to share your insecurities, and you may remember they shared the same ones... At the end of the relationship they knew what buttons to push to extract a reaction from you.

B is for BELITTLING • Put-downs that were MASKED by fake friendliness, advice, or they may have offered you words of "wisdom".

These were designed to make the ABUSER feel better about themselves, making them feel knowledgeable. I have also seen VULTURES use this tactic.

They may have used BELITTLING tactics during the DEVALUATION stage, designed to knock you off the pedestal they had placed you on, they used this technique to make sure you were more invested in the relationship than you were in yourself.

BELITTLING was used to confuse you and to maintain POWER and CONTROL, each time it happened you worked harder to get back and stay on the pedestal.

You were left confused and unsure how to react, you might have found yourself WALKING ON EGGSHELLS, trying to understand what you did wrong. To the outside world they were telling everyone how amazing you were, but behind closed doors those messages were mixed with subtle putdowns and words of conflicting advice.

Nothing made sense.

And now you are left believing this is all your fault, "IF ONLY and MAYBE". Perhaps you are still trying to change your behaviour.

B is for BLAME SHIFTING • BLAME SHIFTING is a tactic used to disguise the ABUSER'S actions, taking the focus off their behaviour.

Because they can never take RESPONSIBILITY for any of their actions, they shifted the BLAME onto you or to another person. This may have sounded like "well if you hadn't done..." or "I wouldn't have to if you..." of course then they wouldn't have behaved or reacted in the way they did.

When your INTUITION was telling you that something was wrong and you tried to discuss it, the conversation transferred to you and your behaviour. You may have found your feelings became minimised.

By playing the VICTIM, they aren't to BLAME for their actions; and it served another purpose, they got the SUPPLY of attention they so desperately needed.

BLAME SHIFTING is used to minimise another person's feelings. They might have used CIRCULAR CONVERSATIONS that left you confused, or they may have guilt-tripped you with their pity stories.

Do you remember the stories they told you about their CRAZY eX, they don't seem so CRAZY now do they? You can now begin to understand what they went through.

Who is the real VICTIM?

You may recognise yourself doing this and ask the QUESTION "AM I THE NARCISSIST?" Are you really BLAME SHIFTING?

Look at the context: are you, or were you WALKING ON EGG SHELLS? Did you deflect the BLAME being put on you in order to protect yourself from being caught out or to deceive another person?

If you were raised by an EMOTIONALLY ABUSIVE parent, it is likely you were taught this technique (see CHILDREN ARE SPONGES and NARCISSISTIC FLEAS), this does not necessarily make you a NARCISSIST, as I mentioned earlier, we are all on the spectrum.

B is for BOUNDARIES • The definition of a BOUNDARY is a line which marks an area; a dividing line. We understand the BOUNDARY that surrounds a property to mark an area. Personal BOUNDARIES are the same, they are the limits we create to keep us safe and the way we will allow other people to behave towards us.

The EMOTIONAL ABUSER understands your BOUNDARIES during the IDEALISATION stage and they very slowly broke them down. They started by pushing against them to see how far they could go and what they could get away with.

You may have told them you weren't happy about their behaviour and they apologised but continued. You may have caught them cheating and they were so sorry. But during this stage they are IDEALISING you and getting you addicted to the hormones that keep you trapped in the relationship. It is done so subtly you don't realise this is what they are doing. No means no: it doesn't mean maybe.

C
is for...
reviveyoursoul.co.uk

Promise me you'll always remember: You're braver than you believe, and stronger than you seem, and smarter than you think.

A.A. Milne

C is for

C is for CIRCULAR CONVERSATIONS • These are arguments which go on endlessly. You believe you have a resolution, but they are resurrected again, repeating the same pattern leaving you confused and exhausted.

If you experienced this, it wasn't about understanding, and it certainly wasn't about compromise, it was about POWER and CONTROL.

I remember feeling drained and confused each time this happened.

There was an initial feeling of relief that we had reached a conclusion, then the conversation would start again. Mentally I would be asking "why?"

I would agree again to the same terms and feeling relief again believing it was over, only to find within hours or the next day it had started again. "But I thought we had agreed" "Yes but..." and off it would go. The same statements, the same conclusions and it wasn't until I was out of the relationship I realised this had been part of the game.

C is for CLOSURE • Relationship CLOSURE involves honest, healthy, non-judgmental communication that helps with letting go. Being denied CLOSURE when you're breaking up is unhealthy; it's damaging, destructive and CONTROLLING.

Relationships break down for different reasons. Healthy people are able to acknowledge what isn't working; it can be painful, but CLOSURE is helpful in moving on for both parties.

But this wasn't a healthy relationship!

The ending of this relationship was painful. The ABUSER created a strong BOND with you during the repeated LOVE BOMBING stage, TRAUMA BONDING you, and when they had drained everything from you, and you were no longer of use to them, they just walked away.

During the DISCARD stage they told you what you did wrong, and their explanation, if you got one, was BLAME SHIFTING, and you were left believing this was all your fault.

This BOND was so strong and the withdrawal so painful, that you looked for ways of getting the relationship back to where you were in the beginning during the IDEALISATION stage.

You might have gone into a spiral of QUESTIONING "what if" and "if only"...

You are trying to understand where you went wrong, replaying situations and conversations - if only you had done something differently or said something else it would it have ended?

Why didn't you get CLOSURE?

There are a few reasons for this. Firstly, they are the VICTIM: it was your behaviour that caused the break-up of the relationship.

The attention they receive from their friends, family, work colleagues, the person next to them on the train, SUPPLIES them, why would they give that up?

Secondly, seeing you in pain is SUPPLYING them with attention, they don't care if it is negative or positive, it's SUPPLY!

All the time you are in pain, confused and asking QUESTIONS, the focus is still on them. They have no EMPATHY; they can't put themselves in your shoes and they don't want to understand the pain you are in.

Knowing that they have caused this pain is the proof they need to show how powerful they are, and reinforces the amount of CONTROL they still have over you.

So, to summarise, giving you CLOSURE would not serve them in any way.

They would be giving up the attention they claim they don't want from you and, they would be handing you back POWER and CONTROL of your life. Another reason would be having to acknowledge that they were somehow to BLAME and they can't do that - their damaged inner child could not handle it.

C is for CLUSTER B PERSONALITY DISORDER • CLUSTER B is a group of characteristics of egocentric people who have difficulty seeing any reason or need to regulate impulses.

PERSONALITY DISORDERS are diagnosed by professionals but because the TOXIC Person or EMOTIONALLY ABUSIVE person can't take RESPONSIBILITY they will never willingly get a diagnosis.

The CLUSTER B PERSONALITY DISORDER[31] is the Dramatic, Emotional, or Erratic Personality Disorders which consist of :

- Antisocial Personality Disorder (ASPD)
- Borderline Personality Disorder (BPD)
- Histrionic Personality Disorder (HPD)
- Narcissistic Personality Disorder (NPD)

Please remember we are all on this scale, as we are on all scales. You might "score" a 3 or a 30, whereas the EMOTIONAL ABUSER or TOXIC person might "score" a 75 or a 90. You may recognise something of yourself, if you feel you have one of these disorders, please go and speak to someone.

C is for CODEPENDENCY • A relationship which is CONTROLLED or MANIPULATED by another. There is an excessive reliance on other people for approval and a sense of identity. Definitions of CODEPENDENCY vary.

An EMOTIONALLY ABUSIVE or TOXIC person MANUFACTURES their actions; the intention was to create desire, JEALOUSY, dependence, addiction, and anxiety.

You made sacrifices for your partner's happiness, perhaps you are only just realising it now.

They did this very slowly, gaining your trust and breaking down your BOUNDARIES (see ENMESHMENT).

Slowly they created the person they believed you were looking for putting on a MASK and playing a character.

They created a FAKE FUTURE with you; they used tactics like TRIANGULATION to create JEALOUSY, making them look popular and wanted. And their favourite tool, COGNITIVE DISSONANCE, which allowed them to manoeuvre themselves into a place of Power and they then started to CONTROL your life.

As children we are CODEPENDENT, we need our parents to provide for our needs. You may have experienced this if a parent was "overprotective", not allowing you healthy BOUNDARIES or the room to grow and mature.

C is for COERCIVE CONTROL • COERCIVE CONTROL is described as an act, or a pattern of assault carried out through forms of threats, humiliation and intimidation.

COERCIVE CONTROL is EMOTIONAL ABUSE, it is used to harm, punish and frighten the VICTIM.

This form of behaviour is used to make the VICTIM dependent on the ABUSER. ISOLATING them from friends and family, they exploit them and deprive them of their independence, regulate their everyday behaviour.

COERCIVE or CONTROLLING behaviour does not relate to one single incident; it is a pattern that occurs over time. Used for one individual to exert POWER and CONTROL over another.

COERCIVE or CONTROLLING behaviour is now a crime in the UK. The law came into force on 29th December 2015. In July 2019 Sally Challen[9] walked free from court which is now being used as a landmark case, that I hope will change the courts' process when dealing with the real VICTIM.

Sally Challen[10] murdered her husband in 2010. At the time of her conviction, COERCIVE CONTROL was not a crime in England and Wales and she was sentenced to life imprisonment. Following the change in the law Justice for Women submitted new grounds of appeal in 2017, these were refused by the judge. In February 2019 Harriet Wistrich[11] asked for Sally's conviction to be overturned. Following the hearing she was released in April on conditional bail. In June 2019, prosecutors accepted Sally's plea of manslaughter. At this stage Sally had served 8 years and 10 months, her retrial was later dropped.

COERCIVE CONTROL creates invisible chains. People might ask why you didn't leave earlier, or why you didn't you see what was going on.

On some level you did know there was something wrong with the relationship. However, during the CYCLE OF ABUSE, there was a point where you lost who you were, and your focus was more about protecting the relationship than protecting yourself.

It was these invisible chains that stopped you from walking away, THE FAKE FUTURE stopped you from moving on. You were waiting for the next hit of OXYTOCIN you received during the LOVE BOMBING.

You found yourself in a world MANUFACTURED by the ABUSER. You found yourself living in confusion and FEAR.

Some common examples[12] of COERCIVE behaviour are:

ISOLATING you from friends and family, monitoring your time • Monitoring you via online communication tools or spyware • Taking CONTROL over aspects of your everyday life, such as where you can go, who you can see, what you can wear and when you can sleep • Depriving you of access to support services, such as medical services • Repeatedly putting you down, such as saying you're worthless • Humiliating, degrading or dehumanising you • CONTROLLING your finances • Making threats or intimidating you •

I have read articles and seen videos saying, "if you're in an ABUSIVE relationship get out".

If you are in an EMOTIONALLY ABUSIVE relationship, it is very likely that you don't realise you are, or invisible chains are holding you there. It would be amazing if it were that simple just to walk away, but it isn't.

And it takes time to untangle from the invisible chains that held you there.

C is for COGNITIVE DISSONANCE • COGNITIVE DISSONANCE occurs when we experience a state of holding two or more contradictory thoughts or beliefs at the same time.

In a relationship, this can be the belief that your partner loves you, but you are experiencing conflict when their behaviour doesn't MIRROR their words. Your INTUITION might have made you feel something was wrong or you didn't believe the story they were telling you. They may have BLAME-SHIFTED and you QUESTIONED yourself believing it was your fault and they may have minimised your feelings. Or they might have tried to confuse you, by saying "but I told you this the other day", and you then recall the conversation running over it again wondering if there is something wrong with your memory.

This form of ABUSE penetrates so many levels, your brain was being tricked to believe what you were told was the truth, it takes time to de-traumatise.

For people healing from a TOXIC relationship, this can cause emotional confusion and anxiety.

COGNITIVE DISSONANCE is the reason people say they feel like they are going CRAZY... A very specific kind of CRAZY!

Eventually, you might have started to wonder what was happening, and believed you couldn't trust your own judgement.

The term GASLIGHTING has been taken from a play written by Patrick Hamilton called *Gaslight*[13] in 1938, which was also made in to a film. The story is about a man who meets a young woman, she falls deeply in love with him, and she believes he feels the same about her (see GASLIGHTING).

When we experience any form of anxiety or go through a prolonged period of stress, our brains go into survival mode; we can't deal with any big decisions, we can barely look after ourselves.

In social situations if your experience is negative or stressful, OXYTOCIN activates a part of the brain that intensifies the memory. Scientists discovered[7] that OXYTOCIN strengthens an important signalling molecule ERK (extracellular signal-regulated kinases), which becomes activated for six hours after a negative social experience, causing enhanced FEAR, stimulating the brain's FEAR pathways.

COGNITIVE DISSONANCE, or GASLIGHTING, is a very unique experience for each individual. Only a person who has gone through this very specific form of ABUSE will understand what it is like, and how deep the trauma runs.

And the worst thing you can say to someone is "get over it", it is like telling someone suffering from depression to cheer up.

If you have experienced this form of ABUSE, it is important to surround yourself with people who understand what you have been through.

For me, understanding what COGNITIVE DISSONANCE and the effects it had on my brain was like waking up from some form of hibernation.

When I understood what I had been through, why my brain couldn't compute, why I was reacting totally out of character, and how this had happened; it was really only the very start of my healing. It was as if someone had turned on a light, and the relief was huge, I wasn't that CRAZY!

I felt the tension leave my body, and this was huge in my own recovery. But it didn't happen overnight, I still had to deal with the TRAUMA BONDING and the EMOTIONAL FLASHBACKS, as well as realising that this wasn't all my fault.

This form of ABUSE penetrates so many levels, so many layers; your brain has been tricked to believe what you were told was the truth, it takes time to de-traumatise. And it is so easy to slip back down the dark hole when faced with new facts and new situations.

When I explain COGNITIVE DISSONANCE, I see a puzzled look as I explain the three stages of EMOTIONAL ABUSE • IDEALISATION • DEVALUATION • DISCARD, and I see clients waking up, a veil has been lifted, I watch them physically change before my eyes!

C is for COMPLEX POST-TRAUMATIC STRESS DISORDER (C-PTSD) • C-PTSD is a psychological INJURY, resulting from repeated trauma over months or years, whereas PTSD is trauma following one single event.

It is not uncommon coming out of an EMOTIONALLY ABUSIVE relationship to experience C_PTSD, you unwittingly entered a war zone, very gradually over a period of time you found yourselves under fire.

At the end of the relationship you may have found yourself reliving the traumatic experience; having nightmares or EMOTIONAL FLASHBACKS. You might be avoiding certain situations, or feel constantly on alert; feeling jittery and easily startled.

Common symptoms[14] of C-PTSD are EMOTIONAL FLASHBACKS, inner or outer critic, TOXIC SHAME, SELF-ABANDONMENT, Social Anxiety, Feelings of LONELINESS and ABANDONMENT, Fragile SELF-ESTEEM, Attachment Disorder, Developmental Arrests, Relationship Difficulties, Radical Mood Swings, Hair TRIGGERED FIGHT/FLIGHT response, Oversensitivity to stressful situations, SUICIDAL IDEATION.

If you are experiencing the signs of C-PTSD creating space in your life is very helpful. You might be constantly looking over your shoulder or wondering if you're being watched through your social media; go outside and ground yourself. Create a safe space within your home, somewhere you feel safe where you can breathe deeply.

Personally for me travel saved me, I didn't realise I was running away constantly but when I was away and on my own I felt something lift, I wasn't looking out for cars when I was driving or looking over my shoulder whilst shopping.

I also created morning and evening routines that took my focus on to me and away from pain I was experiencing.

C is for CONDITIONAL LOVE • CONDITIONAL LOVE is a behaviour displayed by parents to their children. It is a silent language that tells the child they are only LOVEABLE if they behave in a certain way. When the child behaves in that way and they are rewarded with praise and LOVE. If they don't behave in the way their parent expects them to they are punished or any attention is withdrawn.

The message the child receives is LOVE is CONDITIONAL.

This message later translates in their relationships as you will be rewarded with my LOVE when you behave the way I want you to behave.

Unconditional LOVE is the message from a parent to a child saying I LOVE you without limitations.

C is for CRAZY eX • see X is for CRAZY eX

C is for CRAZY MAKING • see Z is for craZy MAKING and COGNITIVE DISSONANCE

D
is for...
reviveyoursoul.co.uk

Shame is the most powerful, master emotion. It's the fear that we're not good enough.

Brene Brown

D is for

D is for DEMENTOR'S KISS • The DEMENTORS are from the Harry Potter stories, they are horrible, faceless, hooded creatures, that feed on human emotions; draining peace, hope, and happiness out of the air around them.

The DEMENTOR'S last weapon is called the DEMENTOR'S KISS[15] where it sucks out a person's Soul, leaving them an empty shell, alive but effectively dead inside.

I used this term to describe what I felt like at the end of one relationship. I remember feeling hollow, a shell of my former self. I felt as if my Soul had been sucked out of me. I had no idea who I was and I felt very little apart from a wounding deep within my Soul.

At the end of the relationship when they had drained you of everything; you had very little to give them the SUPPLY they so desperately need, so they sucked the very last ounce of your essence and walked away.

D is for DETECTIVE • You may have become your own private investigator. Their MASK had slipped, you were no longer a good SUPPLY to them and they became careless. They'd drained you of everything anyway, you were no longer any use to them, so they made no effort to cover their tracks.

Perhaps your INTUITION had kicked in. Their words and actions did not match up. You knew something wasn't right - but you didn't know what it was and when you QUESTIONED them they denied it because although you are not a good SUPPLY they still couldn't take RESPONSIBILITY.

They don't know how to tell the truth; it is so unfamiliar to them, rather than be honest with you they BLAME SHIFTED the situation and you were the problem and it was all your fault.

Have you ever played DETECTIVE before? Probably not!

Your INTUITION was showing you it hadn't ABANDONED you. You are a trusting and rational person, but something inside didn't feel right and you became a super sleuth. You were looking for evidence to validate your feelings, your ABUSER had told you over a period of time you couldn't trust yourself and you were trapped by invisible chains; unable to trust your GUT and walk away.

Why didn't you walk away? Because it was like walking away from a slot machine, you had invested so much of yourself that, in leaving, you might miss out on THE FAKE FUTURE that had been promised. Just like the slot machine, you believed the next coin was going to bring the prize. You believed they really meant it when they said they wouldn't do it again or that they wanted to change for you.

D is for DEVALUATION • During the IDEALISATION stage, you were swept off your feet with the LOVE BOMBING. During the DEVALUATION stage, the ABUSER checked to make sure you were more invested in protecting the relationship than you were in protecting yourself. They did this by making comments about your intelligence or your abilities and perhaps your goals and dreams.

If you QUESTIONED them, they might have told you that you were being oversensitive, or they were only joking!

And these BELITTLING comments and subtle put-downs were followed by IDEALISATION which changed the chemicals in your body (see It causes so much damage). You found yourself addicted, and you over-rode your INTUITION.

During the DEVALUATION stage, they withdrew the attention you received at the start of the relationship, and you accepted any little crumb they threw your way.

They used techniques such as TRIANGULATION.

They may have talked too much about their CRAZY eX or about anyone who gave them attention.

They used this tactic to draw you to them, they created situations that made them look popular so you would fight for their attention. FEARING you would lose the ABUER and the attention you received and not to mention the hormones (see DOPAMINE and OXYTOCIN) that were being released into your body. They created these TRIANGLES as they love to turn people against each other, they kept you just far enough apart so you couldn't compare anything, but close enough to ensure you knew they were a threat.

They MANUFACTURED situations to made you fee JEALOUS and QUESTION their fidelity.

You may have experienced GASLIGHTING where they convinced you that what you were feeling wasn't real, or that you didn't understand the situation, or your facts were wrong; and they were so believable you actually QUESTIONED yourself.

You may have discovered their lies, and they told you, that you were wrong; or you had misunderstood the situation. They possibly told you, you, were just too sensitive or perhaps they accused you of having trust issues.

And you might have QUESTIONED if you were wrong. Did you misunderstand what you had been told? Perhaps you had forgotten what they told you or you weren't listening... This spiral of QUESTIONING can go on for a long time after the relationship is over and takes a long time to untangle from.

Following the DEVALUATION STAGE the ABUSER tested you by DISCARDING you in some way. They did this to make sure you were BONDED to them. They might have disappeared and you were unable to get hold of them. They then reappeared with a gift or compliment, giving you back the feeling you had at the beginning of the relationship and reaffirming that they did love you!

You did notice the cracks in their MASK, but you JUSTIFIED their actions because they kept reaffirming their love for you by taking you back to the LOVE BOMBING stage again and again and again.

D is for DISCARD • In the IDEALISATION STAGE, everything you said and did was watched and noted. You were swept off your feet with the LOVE BOMBING. Then they moved on to the DEVALUATION STAGE, where they started by testing the water, just to make sure they had the programming at the correct setting and, if they'd got it right during the IDEALISATION you would be more interested in protecting the relationship than you were in protecting yourself.

At this point you were addicted, you turned your INTUITION off because apparently, it wasn't working properly... and you were prepared to do anything for your drug of choice, them.

As the attention you received started to disappear, you accepted any little crumb they threw your way.

During the DISCARD STAGE, you experienced the ABUSER withdrawing from you. They weren't as available as they had been, and this pattern continued. Each time they phoned, messaged or became more present in the relationship, they were hooking you back up and reconfirming that you were the love of their life and you were their SOUL MATE. And this pattern continued until...

The FINAL DISCARD.

Your role as SOUL MATE went to your REPLACEMENT, and this is another reason you are in so much pain, you believed in the FAKE FUTURE, you gave them everything they asked for, you did everything they wanted and you gave up so much for them.

Perhaps they had drained you of all your money, and you could no longer support them in the way you did, or you had no energy left to SUPPLY them with the attention they needed and they walked away, you were no longer fit for purpose!

They might have even suggested you were bipolar, and you may have believed this to be true.

If you think back to the time before you met them, were you a normal functioning person in society?

Now think back to the beginning of the relationship, they talked a lot about their old relationships and why they went wrong. They were always the VICTIM, and this relationship will be no different.

The EMOTIONAL ABUSER did the same with you, they were GASLIGHTING you, and then told anyone who would listen that you were CRAZY.

They have poisoned and brainwashed everyone in their lives.

This is about POWER and CONTROL, they can't take RESPONSIBILITY for their actions and if they did they couldn't claim to be the VICTIM and they wouldn't get their SUPPLY.

At the FINAL DISCARD one of two things happened; you started to realise you had to get out of the situation, or they DISCARDED you.

If you were the one to leave, you finally realised you needed to get away; that something was wrong with them and the relationship. On average people go through the DISCARD stage 7-8 times, they keep going back believing the ABUSER will change. And you probably have more CONTROL over your emotions.

If you were DISCARDED it felt like you were going CRAZY, maybe it still does.

The MINDFUCKERY that took place, made you react in ways that were totally out of character.

You possibly ended up showing their FLYING MONKEYS that your ABUSER was right to leave. They left playing the VICTIM, and you gave the ABUSER even more SUPPLY knowing the POWER and CONTROL they still had over you.

If this is exactly how you are feeling at moment, the best thing you can do is hide.

But it is possibly too late; you might have already taken to social media and told the world. You might have sent a barrage of text messages and emails, left voice messages. If you are still in this place, PLEASE stop now!

You may have felt the need to tell everyone "it wasn't me, they did this, this and this". If you are still in this place PLEASE don't do it, they are playing the VICTIM.

The ABUSER claims not to want the attention, but nothing could be further from the truth, they love attention and they love the drama, positive or negative it is SUPPLY.

It doesn't matter if you are still in the relationship, if you have just separated or this happened years ago, your inner child is trying to get your attention and show you where the ORIGINAL WOUND is. The pain you are experiencing, is the withdrawal from the DOPAMINE and OXYTOCIN. This is why you may hear people describe it like coming off heroin.

Try and change your behaviour and use any energy you have left to go inside and find the WOUND that so desperately needs healing.

Do not get sucked back in, this is a game, and they love to HOOVER. It gives them the SUPPLY of attention they so desperately need, proves to them how powerful they still are, and they enjoy seeing and hearing how broken you are.

I remember trying to go NO CONTACT and getting a message saying how difficult that was going to be, that we should be together, we were SOULMATES...

I remember thinking I have got this all wrong he does love me! BUT when I tried to make contact, I was told he was turning his phone off in the evening and overnight as he was so busy at work and needed the space to clear his head... imintheflow

At the end of one of my relationships, I realised I didn't appear on the list of important people in his life, who needed his attention.

PLEASE, PLEASE, PLEASE

If you feel you do have a mental health condition, please seek help! The techniques they used damage your brain. You might be on hyper-alert, and they are not going to give you the CLOSURE you need to help you move on.

D is for DOPAMINE • DOPAMINE is the hormone RESPONSIBLE for the brain's reward centre. And a lot of research has been carried out on the DOPAMINE pathway and addiction.

The same regions that light up when we are attracted to someone light up if you were to take cocaine. And the same brain regions also light up when we become addicted to material goods as well as when we become emotionally dependent on our partners.

You may hear people describe the emotions at the end of a relationship are like an addict going into withdrawal.

Too much DOPAMINE in a relationship can underlie unhealthy emotional dependence on your partner.

E
is for...
reviveyoursoul.co.uk

One life is all we have and we live it as we believe in living it. But to sacrifice what you are and to live without belief, that is a fate more terrible than dying.

Joan of Arc

E is for

E is for ECHOISM • ECHOISTS[17] tend to fall into relationships with extremely NARCISSISTIC partners and friends.

In Greek mythology[16] Echo was a very talkative Wood Nymph. One afternoon she came across Hera who was out looking for her husband (and brother) Zeus. Zeus was entertaining some Wood Nymphs and Echo distracted Hera, which allowed him to get away.

Realising what had happened, Hera punished Echo by taking away her voice, she was only able to repeat whatever she heard.

One day Echo came across Narcissus, she immediately fell in love with him, but because of the curse, she couldn't say anything, she had to wait for him to speak.

When Narcissus saw Echo, he rejected her, so she went and hid in a cave. She stayed there and eventually she withered away, leaving only her voice.

Narcissus had broken many hearts, one of these rejected women appealed to the gods. And Nemesis, the goddess of vengeance, responded.

One day, Narcissus came across a clearing with a silver pool. He knelt to take a drink and caught sight of himself and fell in love with his own reflection.

Narcissus started talking to it, telling himself how amazing he was and how many nymphs and young girls had fallen in love with him.

So obsessed with his reflection, he eventually wasted away from hunger. When the Nymphs went to bury his body, they only found a flower.

Like Echo, people who struggle with ECHOISM struggle to have a voice of their own.

They're afraid of being a burden and berate themselves for being too needy. In the mild range of ECHOISM, these are people who can be deeply EMPATHIC. They prefer to focus on others as opposed to themselves.

People who have been raised by extremely NARCISSISTIC parents are vulnerable to this.

E is for EMOTIONAL ABUSE • EMOTIONAL ABUSE is a pattern of behaviour: one person uses fear, humiliation, guilt or MANIPULATION tactics to gain POWER over another.

Unlike physical ABUSE it often goes unnoticed, and the damage it causes puts you into a state of confusion, you had no idea it was taking place; and like Chinese water torture, it happened very slowly and turned you CRAZY. They chipped away at your SELF-ESTEEM, and you began to doubt your perceptions and reality.

The CYCLE OF ABUSE is EMOTIONAL ABUSE. The ABUSER used many tactics to trap you and to gain POWER and CONTROL over you, your life and your finances.

They MANIPULATED you into believing they were protecting you, when in fact they were ABUSING you.

E is for EMOTIONAL FLASHBACKS • EMOTIONAL FLASHBACKS[14] are sudden and overwhelming feelings TRIGGERING your survival instincts (see THE FOUR F's).

These emotions can include FEAR, SHAME, ALIENATION, RAGE, grief and depression. EMOTIONAL FLASHBACKS can range from subtle to horrific, and they vary in duration from moments to weeks (see C-PTSD).

This is one of the reasons it is so important to go NO CONTACT, or GREY ROCK. By being in contact with the ABUSER you are still on alert, your body needs time to detach from them.

E is for EMOTIONAL INTELLIGENCE • This is the ability to recognise and regulate your own emotions and to demonstrate EMPATHY for how others around you feel.

You are able to understand the consequences of your actions and regulate your behaviour.

E is for EMPATH • An EMPATH has the ability to sense the emotions of others.

They are sensitive to the visible as well as the invisible, intuitively picking up on body language and tone of voice.

EMPATHS understand what is being said, as well as what is not being said. And they are sensitive to other people's energies.

E is for ENABLER • The ENABLER is a person who attempts to pacify another, they sacrifice their own or another's needs, in an attempt to keep the peace.

(see FAWNING and THE FOUR F's).

The ENABLER supports the EMOTIONAL ABUSER or TOXIC person, defending them, they are also known as FLYING MONKEYS. There are ENABLERS, who might not agree with the EMOTIONAL ABUSER or what they do, but they put up with their behaviour.

They follow them around clearing up the mess the ABUSER causes. They believe they are helping, but their actions are telling the ABUSER what they have done is OK.

E is for ENMESHED • ENMESHMENT is a dysfunctional state where two or more people have poor BOUNDARIES. ENMESHMENT can occur between a parent and child, whole families, or adult couples.

Very slowly during the IDEALISATION stage, they told you how amazing you were, they put on a MASK and played the character they had so carefully extracted from you. They very slowly broke down your BOUNDARIES, pushing against them to see how far they could go and what they could get away with.

You saw the RED FLAGS, and you challenged their behaviour, but they were so persuasive you believed their answers.

And very slowly they had eroded your BOUNDARIES, and you became dependent on them. You were ENMESHED and your identity was eroded.

This is one of the reasons why you feel so awful coming out of the relationship, you don't know who you are, you've lost your self and your self-worth.

E
is for...
reviveyoursoul.co.uk

We think sometimes that poverty is only being hungry, naked and homeless. The poverty of being unwanted, unloved and uncared for is the greatest poverty. We must start in our own homes to remedy this kind of poverty.

Mother Teresa

F is for

F is for FAKE TEARS • Also known as Crocodile Tears. Perhaps you found the ABUSER crying over a situation or using tears to MANIPULATE your feelings. I found myself in two relationships and a friendship where this happened. The first time I was young and had no idea what was going on, someone else called him out, and I watched the ABUSER jump off the floor and walk away.

I have since then realised my internal guidance tells me if they are fake. So now I listen. If I hear "really?", or "are you kidding me", I know the tears are fake. When I see real tears, my eyes leak, or I feel their pain in my heart.

F is for FEAR • FEAR is a feeling induced by perceived danger or threat (see FOUR F's).

FEAR in these relationships is a feeling of loss and a deep emptiness; your brain isn't working and you cannot compute anything.

You were programmed over months and years to believe you needed the ABUSER to survive and that anyone else was a threat to you and your safety.

And then one day they walked away.

You have no idea how you are going to survive without them.

You may even realise that you had a life before you met them, and wonder why you are experiencing so much FEAR and not know how to live. The stress hormones are RAGING around your body and to protect itself from the trauma, your brain went into hibernation.

Their insecurities and their FEARS were PROJECTED onto you.

There was a type of bartering that went on which you were unaware of. Instead of it being an even swap where you both benefitted, you had something they wanted so they took it, and they had an insecurity, or something they didn't like about themselves so they gave it to you.

Their biggest FEAR is ABANDONMENT and they do everything to strip you of your SELF-ESTEEM and make you FEARFUL of them ABANDONING you.

The emotion is indescribable but it is due to the GASLIGHTING and COGNITIVE DISSONANCE, which transpires in FEAR.

Or you may feel LONELY and in pain as you watch your REPLACEMENT step into your FAKE FUTURE. This feeling could be due to the TRAUMA BONDING that took place, and the FEAR of not knowing how to function without them. They manoeuvred themselves into your life putting themselves into a place of POWER, and then they took CONTROL of you. They were so insecure they actually FEARED you would leave them, so they made you believe you couldn't function without them.

And they kept reminding you how lucky you were to have them.

When you were no longer of use to them, they left without a backward glance. You were left with EMOTIONS that were completely unfamiliar to you and living in FEAR.

You have lost everything; you need time to grieve. You are grieving the relationship, THE FAKE FUTURE and the SOUL MATE.

This LONELINESS may bring up feelings of being unworthy. They moved on and during the DEVALUATION stage, they told you time and time again what was wrong with you.

You may have found you not only lost yourself emotionally, mentally, physically and spiritually in the relationship, but you also lost your finances.

This LONELINESS is a pain that emanates from deep within your Soul, you can barely function, and you don't understand who you have become, and if the real you is still in there.

The pain you are experiencing are old WOUNDS, and I hope one day you will realise the gift they have given you, the chance to heal.

Perhaps this isn't what you are feeling at the moment, and you are desperately holding yourself back from trying to re-engage with them, the pain of being out of this relationship may feel worse than the pain of being in it.

On average, people go back seven to eight times, and I believe FEAR is one of the reasons.

F is for FLYING MONKEYS • Also known as the Entourage or Accomplices. FLYING MONKEYS[18] are ENABLERS, they are an extension of the EMOTIONAL ABUSER. The term "FLYING MONKEYS" comes from the Wizard of Oz[19], they were the brainwashed minions used by Wicked Witch of the West.

As well as being used to boost the ABUSER'S ego, FLYING MONKEYS are also used for spying and in SMEAR CAMPAIGNS.

They spy on you and your social media accounts, reporting back information.

Ensure you secure all your accounts, change your passwords and, if you can, use 2-step verification, where a text message is sent to you, if someone tries to access your account you are notified.

F is for FUTURE FAKING • The future you created together was MANUFACTURED during the IDEALISATION stage when they listened to your every word and watched your every move, possibly stalking your social media accounts. Nothing about that FUTURE was real, but the stories around it were so believable.

And they took just enough of your dreams for the future, which they intertwined in to THE FAKE FUTURE they created with you, so you believed they were as invested in the relationship as you were.

You need to grieve the future as well as the loss of the relationship.

You believed in it, and you gave up so much of yourself.

You stayed in the relationship for too long - just like the slot machine; too afraid of walking away, the promise of the future held you there.

G
is for...
reviveyoursoul.co.uk

I simply can't build my hopes on a foundation of confusion, misery and death... I think... peace and tranquillity will return again.

Anne Frank

G is for

G is for GASLIGHTING • A covert way of distorting another person's perception of reality; making them QUESTION their sanity and their memory (see COGNITIVE DISSONANCE). This is CRAZY-MAKING, it makes you think that you're actually going CRAY, CRAY (craziness at a whole different level).

You can't trust yourself, or your perception of reality.

You start to believe the ABUSER'S version of events, and slowly they begin to take over your life.

GASLIGHTING was used to make you feel something was wrong with you. They used tactics to deflect from their behaviour, making you feel you were mentally unstable, or that you were overreacting.

For people healing from these TOXIC relationships, this can cause emotional confusion and anxiety (see C-PTSD).

Eventually, you may have started to wonder what was happening, and that you couldn't trust your own judgement.

The term GASLIGHTING comes from a play written by Patrick Hamilton called *Gaslight*[13] in 1938, which was also made into a film. The story is about a man who meets a young woman, she falls deeply in love with him, and she believes he feels the same about her. He then starts to play with her mind. The wife, Bella, gets upset with her husband's unexplained disappearances and his failure to tell her where he is going increases her anxiety. Her husband, Jack, makes her believe she is going CRAZY and used this form of MANIPULATION on the people around her as well; they believed, just like his wife, that he is protecting her.

Her husband systematically MANIPULATED her, and the term "GASLIGHTING" is now commonly used to describe this MANIPULATIVE behaviour.

When you experience any form of anxiety or go through a prolonged period of stress, your brain goes into survival mode; you can't make decisions, you can barely look after yourself.

GASLIGHTING or COGNITIVE DISSONANCE is a very unique experience for each individual.

This was very different from a normal break-up, be it romantic, a friendship, with a family member or work colleague. Only a person who has gone through this very specific form of ABUSE will understand what it is like and how deep the trauma runs.

For me, understanding what COGNITIVE DISSONANCE was, and the effects it had on my brain was like waking up from some form of deep hibernation. The state your brain works from has been described as a fog, and I felt the fog lifting slightly.

When I understood what I had been through; why my brain couldn't compute, why I was so forgetful and why I wasn't able to retain any information, why I was reacting totally out of character, and how this had happened; it was really the very start of my healing.

It was as if someone had turned on a light, and the relief was huge, I remember thinking I wasn't THAT crazy!

I could literally feel the tension leave my body, it was a milestone in my own recovery, and I was able to cut away some of the invisible chains that still had a hold over me

I kept replaying the same scenarios over and over in my mind and asking the same QUESTIONS "What if" and "If only". I was able to replay the events and situations that didn't match-up. The weird excuses and how I was JEALOUS, and I had trust issues. Understanding the CYCLE OF ABUSE, the GASLIGHTING and other tactics that were used, helped me to make sense of everything.

This form of ABUSE penetrates so many levels, so many layers; your brain was been tricked to believe what you were told was the truth. It takes time to de-traumatise, and it is so easy to slip back down the dark hole when faced with new facts or new situations. You were never going to get the CLOSURE you needed and that is part of the game.

GASLIGHTING is really dangerous, creating the feelings of Insecurity, Confusion, Brain Fog, Self-doubt, Fear, Not Feeling Good Enough, Feeling Vulnerable or Powerless.

G is for GHOSTING • GHOSTING is a technique used during the DISCARD stage. Again like GASLIGHTING this word is appearing more regularly in television shows and articles.

You might have experienced the ABUSER withdrawing from you, or they just disappeared. They may not have been as available as they once were, and this pattern repeated until the FINAL DISCARD. This was another tool they used to gain POWER and CONTROL over you.

They used this to BOND you to the relationship, and each time they phoned, messaged, or became more present in the relationship, they were hooking you back up.

You believed they were re-confirming you were the love of their life, as they started LOVE BOMBING you again and this continued until either you left, or they DISCARDED you.

When they decided the relationship was over, they stopped communicating with you. This leaves you feeling confused and wondering what happened and what you did wrong.

GHOSTING is common in SHORT RELATIONSHIPS where they just disappear and you are left wondering what happened.

G is for GOLDEN CHILD V SCAPEGOAT • This is common in EMOTIONALLY ABUSIVE families. The GOLDEN CHILD is the "best" child in the eyes of the ABUSIVE Parent. The GOLDEN CHILD is the child that the Parent gives more attention to as they make the parent look good. The child might excel in a sport or academically and through association the parent is able to brag about their achievements, which gains them their SUPPLY.

The SCAPEGOAT, on the other hand, can do nothing right, and they take the BLAME for others' wrongdoing.

The parent picks one child as the SCAPEGOAT and another as the GOLDEN CHILD and they play their games through TRIANGULATION. The children are pitted against each other and in some instances the GOLDEN CHILD is actively encouraged to gang up against the SCAPEGOAT.

The message the GOLDEN CHILD receives from the relationship is one of CONDITIONAL LOVE. The child is only worthy of love by behaving is a certain way and is rejected if they don't perform.

G is for GREY ROCK • A technique that can be used when you aren't able to do NO CONTACT, it might be because of children, or a family member, or work colleague.

Become as interesting as a GREY ROCK. Stop being a source of SUPPLY for their drama and attention, they will become bored and move on.

Your relationship was about POWER and CONTROL, and this is a way of claiming it back. Your ABUSER thrives on knowing they still have CONTROL over you, so being as interesting as a GREY ROCK, you are not reacting or giving any information away.

Use neutral language and tone; if you need to have a conversation talk about boring subjects, do not reveal anything going on in your life. Think of the most boring character you know, take on their persona and play that role. And do not engage with them on any level, especially emotionally. Use YES and NO answers, and don't make any effort for them; as well as not being interesting with your language you can take it further with your appearance.

If they see you upset or angry at something they have done, you are feeding them. DO NOT FEED THE ANIMALS!

Think of them like an electric car that needs charging up before you can use it, each time you react you are giving them this SUPPLY.

G is for GUT FEELING · see INTUITION

H
is for...
reviveyoursoul.co.uk

I don't like to give advice. I like to give people information because everyone's life is different, and everyone's journey is different.

Dolly Parton

H is for

H is for HEALTHY NARCISSISM • Children are naturally NARCISSISTIC, with a need for attention and praise. On the climbing frame they may shout "Look at me!" or they come out of school smiling "Look what I did today!".

A healthy parent validates a child's unique qualities, boosting their SELF-ESTEEM and establishing a sense of self-love.

There is a diversity of thought over the term HEALTHY NARCISSISM[20], QUESTIONING how NARCISSISM can be healthy.

The term HEALTHY NARCISSISM is used by some to describe the understanding that you are separate from other people and you don't see them as OBJECTS. Understanding you are RESPONSIBLE for your own happiness and having healthy SELF-ESTEEM. And having the confidence to express your needs, taking the steps needed to have them met without MANIPULATING others.

H is for HOOKED • When I use the term HOOKED it is to describe the process of HOOKING you and keeping you in the relationship to be dependent on the ABUSER.

In the CYCLE OF ABUSE they play the role of the fisherman patiently waiting at the side of a river or lake waiting for a bite. The fisherman casts out their line with the bait attached, when they feel a tug on the line they don't try to land the fish straight away. Instead, they allow the fish to swim away, giving it a false sense of security, but all the time the HOOK is in its mouth, and once they feel the fish is HOOKED, the fisherman starts to reel in the line and then they land it.

During the relationship you were programmed. Everything you experienced was everything you were looking for, and that is why it was so hard to let go, just as the person standing at the slot machine finds it hard to walk away so did you, you had invested so much, even though you saw the RED FLAGS.

They HOOKED you up to OXYTOCIN and DOPAMINE and like a drug addict, at the end of the relationship you are trying to get your fix. During the CYCLE OF ABUSE they created drama and situations where you learnt to fight for their attention and you were rewarded. When the relationship ended you are left with feelings of LONELINESS and LOW SELF-ESTEEM, wondering what is wrong with your and what you did wrong.

H is for HOOVERING • The term used to describe being "sucked back in" following a DISCARD. Just like a vacuum cleaner, the ABUSER attempts to get you back.

This was used during the DISCARD stage, to hook you back into the relationship, ensuring you were more focused on protecting the relationship than you were on yourself.

You might have been HOOVERED when you started to see who they really were, and what was going on. Or maybe you were QUESTIONING their behaviour, realising it wasn't healthy. Perhaps when you were asking for guidance from your friends and family.

You might have experienced HOOVERING at the end of the relationship if they sensed you were moving on. Like a vampire, they came back in an attempt to hook you back in or drain you of the energy you had gained from being away from them.

You are an OBJECT to the ABUSER, something that they initially desired; so now they believe you belong to them and no one else is allowed to have you.

They changed their behaviour, which gave you a false sense of security. They allowed you to believe they really did love you, that they want you back and they are still the person you first met, your (MANUFACTURED) SOUL MATE.

I
is for...
reviveyoursoul.co.uk

Your vision will become clear only when you can look into your own heart. Who looks outside, dreams; who looks inside, awakes.

Carl Jung

I is for

I is for IDEALISATION • The technique that is also known as LOVE BOMBING is the first stage in the CYCLE OF ABUSE.

At the very beginning of the relationship, everything you said and did was watched and noted. They swept you off your feet with compliments, gifts, days and meals out, your every need was catered for: this was deliberate. The text messages they sent early in the morning ensured they were the first thing you thought about, and again at the end of the day, so you went to bed thinking about them. It allowed them to MANUFACTURE a relationship where you had so much in common; you shared the same hopes and dreams and had the same insecurities. They told you that no one had ever understood them and you were SOULMATES.

They may have said[21]:

"We have so much in common."

"We have the same hopes and dreams."

"We share the same insecurities."

"You are Beautiful."

"I've never felt this way in my life."

"We are SOULMATES."

Do any of these sound familiar?

They listened and MIRRORED what was important to you, and they repeated these back as if they were their own.

And, as part of that process, they began not only to take over your life but also your future. They created a BOND that was later to become so hard to let go of.

They created a FAKE FUTURE with you. Nothing about it was real, but the stories around it were so believable, and you were there planning it with them.

You shared the same insecurities, and of course, they told you many times about the awful childhood they had.

You listened to them and helped them. And they praised you, but you may have wondered who was going to help you or when it was your turn.

You were boosted higher onto the pedestal, and you were told that no one had ever understood them the way you did. They had never met anyone like you, you were amazing!

You are amazing! But what they were really saying was; how amazing you were putting them at the centre of your world. How amazing you were to put their needs first and how amazing you were to focus on them.

The compliments you received from them made you feel special.

"You are so Beautiful!"

They may have compared you to their exes. What was actually happening; they were training you to SUPPLY them with compliments. And they were also instilling at the same time, that you needed to look nice for them, to impress them.

They told you they had never met anyone like you; you were so special! When they compared you to their exes, they were affirming to you that they exes for a reason. They were covertly telling you, that if you wanted to stay in this relationship, you'd better not do what they had done, or you would be one in that long line of CRAZY eXes...

You didn't QUESTION what the common denominator was in these relationships.

"We are meant to be together. We are SOULMATES!" They love the idea of being a romantic; they love the attention it gives them. They were creating a BOND; the more they talked about it, the more you started to believe them.

Think about it; you had so much in common, you were starting to map out your FAKE FUTURE together! They were the person of your dreams. "You are beautiful" and "You are the only person (so far) that has really understood me".

Of course, you were SOULMATES!

And you were HOOKED - it was that simple (for them).

I is for INTUITION • You have an ancient warning system in your body, referred to as a GUT FEELING, or INTUITION. It is there to protect you from harm.

During the IDEALISATION stage, it was overridden. You started to QUESTION the messages you were receiving; you were told you had got something wrong or misunderstood what they had meant. You then started to QUESTION these GUT FEELINGS and believed that they were wrong.

If something feels wrong, it usually is, listen to your GUT.

You were told you had misunderstood your INTUITION because they didn't want to be caught out, **not** because your feeling was wrong.

I is for ISOLATION • You were ISOLATED from your friends and family.

The EMOTIONAL ABUSER believed you were their possession; they resented the time you spent with others and the importance you put on those relationships, including the ones with your children.

The EMOTIONAL ABUSER ISOLATED you from your support network, they couldn't risk you confiding in anyone else, so they made up stories to discredit them. They did this to protect themselves; if your friends or family had approached you with any concerns you would QUESTION their motives and reliability rather than the EMOTIONAL ABUSER'S.

You may have ISOLATED yourself following the IDEALISATION stage, believing you had found this amazing creature who had walked into your life, who you wanted to spend as much time with as possible. Or you may have ISOLATED yourself because part of you knew if you did tell anyone what had happened in the relationship, they would have confirmed your fears that this wasn't a healthy relationship. And during the CYCLE OF ABUSE they were ensuring you were more invested in the relationship that you were in protecting yourself. They also told you repeatedly how lucky you were to have a person like them in your life.

You were HOOKED on your drug of choice and weren't able to give it up (see We are all a Bunch of Chemicals).

At the end of the relationship, you may find yourself ISOLATED because you withdrew from friends and family.

J
is for...
reviveyoursoul.co.uk

You gain strength, courage, and confidence by every experience in which you really stop to look fear in the face. You are able to say to yourself, "I lived through this horror. I can take the next thing that comes along."

Eleanor Roosevelt

J is for

J is for JEALOUSY • To be JEALOUS is to be upset and angry because someone that you love seems interested in another person or because someone has something you want.

You might feel JEALOUS if you FEAR you are about to lose something or someone.

Children can become JEALOUS if they perceive their parents love and attention is going to other people. If there is more than one child in the home it can appear as sibling rivalry causing angst between children over toys and attention.

But JEALOUSY in these relationships is different; it was MANUFACTURED for the purpose of causing emotion and attachment. The EMOTIONAL ABUSER used techniques like TRIANGULATION to create JEALOUSY. They wanted you to be JEALOUS of other people, it was part of their game. In order to take CONTROL of your life they needed to crush your SELF-ESTEEM. They create JEALOUSY in the relationship as part of the TRAUMA BONDING and MINDFUCKERY to make believe you are going CRAZY and they then BLAME SHIFT telling your it is all your fault, you have trust issues.

This is done for their benefit. It turns the focus on them, remember it does not matter where the attention comes from or whether it is negative or positive; in their mind is a simple mathematical equation; attention equals SUPPLY.

J is for JUSTIFICATION • Most people have inner guidance that lets them know what is right and wrong, and they understand that there can be consequences to their actions.

When someone is JUSTIFYING their behaviour, they are trying to "get away" with something, and they use BLAME SHIFTING because "it's not their fault".

They rationalise their decisions and behaviour. I believe they know what they are doing is wrong, or that it will hurt the people they claim to care about. But because they believe they are entitled they JUSTIFY it to themselves. And when caught, they revert to the age when their small child was TRAUMATISED and they JUSTIFY why it is not their fault, they cannot take RESPONSIBILITY for their actions.

"You made me do it..."

K
is for...
reviveyoursoul.co.uk

Trauma isn't what happens to you.
It's what happens inside you.

Dr. Gabor Mate

K is for

K is for masKing • They play different roles for different people and use MASKS to cover who they really are.

At the beginning of the relationship, while you were being IDEALISED, you were disclosing details about yourself and what you were looking for in a relationship. Everything you said and did was heard and noted, they then went to work creating that character, they do this because of their LOW SELF-ESTEEM.

To some degree, we all wear MASKS from time to time; perhaps when we are trying to make a good impression, meeting new people or going for an interview. And you may use a different language when talking with different people, perhaps you have a telephone voice. If you are in contact with friends from school, think about the way you behave with them in comparison with other friendship groups.

Over a period of time you may have noticed the way the ABUSER spoke to you changed. Perhaps they used different words or a different style of language. I remember asking one, "where did you learn these words?" when he started to sound like a counsellor.

I was no longer a good source of SUPPLY, he was in a transition stage, although the MASK was dropping, he couldn't risk me DISCARDING him.

Either his next source of SUPPLY hadn't been fully secured, or very possibly the language was coming from a short-term relationship.

You might have noticed a change in the way they dressed, or perhaps their taste in food changed.

When they let their MASK slip, you were no longer SUPPLYING them with the attention they needed. They had drained you of everything, and perhaps you had run out of money and could no longer support them, or there was a new prospect on the horizon who had access to more finances than you could provide, higher salary, newer cars or a nicer home.

So they became careless and didn't feel they had to make such an effort to keep you securely in place, they knew they had BONDED you enough so if the relationship didn't work they could HOOVER you back.

You may have seen a glimpse of the person they really are when they were dealing with other people; you probably thought "that won't happen to me", possibly because you were the only person who has ever understood them, remembering their other exes didn't.

Sadly the way they treated others was an indication of how they would eventually treat you.

L
is for...
reviveyoursoul.co.uk

My mission in life is not merely to survive, but to thrive; and to do so with some passion, some compassion, some humour, and some style.

Maya Angelou

L is for

L is for LONELINESS • Perhaps you feel very LONELY or empty inside. LONELINESS after being in an EMOTIONALLY ABUSIVE relationship could be for many reasons, you were more focused on protecting your relationship than you were protecting yourself.

There is nothing left of you, it feels like your Soul has been sucked out of you. Just like the DEMENTOR'S KISS during the FINAL DISCARD or following the HOOVERING, you feel dead inside.

When you finally find the courage to talk about what happened; you might find there is no one around to listen to you, or you have the wrong people around you, or you may find a VULTURE arrives.

During your relationship, you might have been ISOLATED from friends and family. Perhaps it was due to TRIANGULATION, making you feel JEALOUS, QUESTIONING everything.

Or you may feel LONELY and in pain as you watched your REPLACEMENT step into your FAKE FUTURE. This feeling could be due to the TRAUMA BONDING that took place, and the FEAR of not knowing how to function without them. They manoeuvred themselves into your life putting themselves into a place of POWER, and then they took CONTROL of you. They were so insecure they actually FEARED you would leave them, so they made you believe you couldn't function without them.

And they kept reminding you how lucky you were to have them.

When you were no longer of use to them, they left without a backward glance. You were left with emotions that were completely unfamiliar to you and living in FEAR.

Those around you may be confused as to why it takes you so long for you to move on. You may even hear people ask why you just can't get over it, I know I did, one comment was "shouldn't you be over this by now?"

Unless you have experienced this type of relationship, you will never understand the pain and deep loss.

This ABUSE was done so insidiously it takes a long time to untangle from the invisible chains.

Everything you believed to be true is now turning out to be a lie.

You have lost everything; you need time to grieve. You are grieving THE FAKE FUTURE and the SOUL MATE.

This LONELINESS may bring up feelings of being unworthy, they have moved and during the DEVALUATION stage, they told you time and time again what was wrong with you.

You may have found you have not only lost yourself emotionally, mentally, physically and spiritually in the relationship, but you also lost your finances and being barely able to survive, proving to you that you weren't able to survive without them.

This LONELINESS is a pain that emanates from deep within your Soul, you can barely function, and you don't understand who you have become, and if the real you is still in there.

There is a gift that will come from this, and that gift is the feeling of being whole.

The pain you are experiencing, are old wounds, and I hope one day you will realise the gift they have given you, the chance to heal.

Perhaps this isn't what you are feeling at the moment, and every ounce of you is holding yourself back from trying to re-engage with them, the pain of being out of this relationship may feel worse than the pain of being in it.

On average, people go back seven to eight times, and I believe FEAR is one of the reasons. Wanting to believe they will change as they HOOVER you back up, with promises and feelings you had during the IDEALISATION stage making you feel safe again.

L is for LOVE BOMBING • IDEALISATION is also known as LOVE BOMBING, the first stage in the CYCLE OF ABUSE. At the very beginning of the relationship, everything you said and did was watched and noted. They swept you off your feet with compliments, gifts, days and meals out, your every need was catered for, and this was deliberate.

The text messages early in the morning ensured they were the first thing you thought about and also at the end of the day, so you went to bed thinking about them.

It allowed them to MANUFACTURE a relationship where you had so much in common; shared the same hopes and dreams and had the same insecurities, all of which you shared early on in the relationship and they later used against you during the DISCARD stage. The LOVE BOMBING was the place you wanted to get back to when the cycle moved to the DEVALUATION and then the DISCARD stages and each time you went back to this stage, you felt secure again.

L is for LOW SELF-ESTEEM • LOW SELF-ESTEEM is a lack of confidence and a fragile sense of self that can easily be wounded by others.

When you come out of an EMOTIONALLY ABUSIVE relationship, it can leave you with feelings of being unlovable and hypersensitivity. You become your most severe critic, berating yourself constantly.

You were BONDED during the IDEALISATION stage, and then during the DEVALUATION stage you were told what was wrong with **you**, and this was done so slowly and insidiously, you believed this is all your fault. And you then repeated the criticism in your mind.

You were tricked in to believing this was all your fault, it was part of the game. They needed to you provide the attention for their own damaged SELF-ESTEEM to make them feel good and they couldn't risk losing you so they keep you trapped in the relationship with COERCIVE techniques. You are left on the floor, a shell of your former self QUESTIONING everything and asking what you did wrong.

To overcome LOW SELF-ESTEEM, you need to start challenging your thoughts, and listen carefully to the voice in your head, is it yours?

If it isn't yours, whose is it? Listen closely you may recognise it...

Start challenging these statements (see Befriending your PFF at the end of the book).

M
is for...
reviveyoursoul.co.uk

The problem is, fairytales don't come true. It's the nightmares that always seem to become the reality.

Meredith Grey

M is for

M is for MANIPULATION • ABUSERS are MASTERS of MANIPULATION, they use words to deceive, COERCE, seduce, and mislead to gain POWER and CONTROL.

So basically, if their lips are moving, it is a lie and if you don't believe me start to look at the things they told you, are they true?

They told you they loved you and you were SOULMATES, was this true?

They told you they were the VICTIM in all their relationships was this true?

Break things down and it might start to help you untangle from the invisible chains that held you in the relationship far longer than you should have stayed.

M is for MANUFACTURED EMOTIONS • These are emotions that are not entirely familiar, you have felt them before, but these were MANUFACTURED for a purpose.

They created situations that heightened your feelings of JEALOUSY, neediness, RAGE, anxiety, doubt and insecurity. They were carefully MANUFACTURED.

You may have never considered yourself to be a particularly JEALOUS person, but in this relationship, you experienced emotions very unfamiliar to you, and when you said anything, they BLAME SHIFTED and you were told it was all your fault. These emotions were MANUFACTURED from the TRIANGULATION, GHOSTING, DEVALUATION, TRAUMA BONDING that took place. Your ABUSER is a very insecure person, and they needed to make sure you were HOOKED, to ensure you were not going to ABANDON them.

This was a game, they love playing with people's Emotions, they love to see how much CONTROL they can gain over everyone. And this started really early in the relationship. Little baby steps to see if you would move your BOUNDARIES because if you did, they knew they could just keep pushing at them.

M is for MASKING • see K is for masKing •They play different roles for different people, they put on a MASK and played the role of the person who they believed you were looking for. You saw the RED FLAGS, and you saw their MASK slip, it could have been that you were no longer a good SUPPLY of attention, they became careless and didn't feel they had to make such an effort.

Or you might have had a glimpse of the person they really are when they were dealing with other people, believing they would never do that to you, why would they when you are the only person who had ever understood them.

M is for MINDFUCKERY • *Definition noun. Vulgar Slang.* The term used to describe mental confusion inflicted deliberately by another person. When the words used don't match the action "but he says he loves me, why would he do that".

MINDFUCKERY is the collision of COGNITIVE DISSONANCE and GASLIGHTING.

It is the mental confusion that happens in such a covert way that it distorts your reality, making you QUESTION your sanity and your memory. It is CRAZY-MAKING.

Your INTUITION told you something was wrong or you didn't believe the story they were telling you. They lied to you and you ended up QUESTIONING yourself, whilst they minimised your feelings.

The little seahorses (see It causes so much damage...) went into hibernation, protecting you from further damage to your brain. Our bodies have an amazing way of protecting us.

Long-term contact with a TOXIC or EMOTIONALLY ABUSIVE person causes damage to the brain.

M is for MIRRORING • MIRRORING allows the EMOTIONAL ABUSER to MANUFACTURE a relationship where you had so much in common, you shared the same hopes and dreams and had the same insecurities. You were told that no one had ever understood them the way you did, and you were SOULMATES.

They were MIRRORING all your amazing qualities, all the things they have missing, the EMPATHY and caring for others. Your inner beauty and your deep forgiving Soul!

I believe these people are insecure and are looking for constant validation. I don't know if they realise how much damage and hurt they cause, or if they in fact care. It is really sad, but it doesn't make their behaviour right, so forgive them, and now make yourself the priority.

I want you to consider this, what if part of you fell in love with yourself? I know you are hurting and have been for a long time, but NOW is the time to fall back in LOVE with you! You are an amazing person!

N
is for...
reviveyoursoul.co.uk

People always say that I didn't give up my seat because I was tired, but that isn't true. I was not tired physically... No, the only tired I was, was tired of giving in.

Rosa Parks

N is for

N is for NARCISSIST • A person who behaves in a selfish way, with a grandiose sense of importance, and an insatiable need for admiration, wealth, POWER or fame.

They lack EMPATHY and consideration for others.

NARCISSISTS feel entitled to special treatment, they are easily offended and readily harbour grudges. However, they are often very popular, until you are no longer of use to them and they DISCARD you.

They are children in an adult's body, unable to take RESPONSIBILITY for any of their actions, and anyone who disagrees with them or their unreasonable expectations might be subjected to their NARCISSISTIC RAGE. There are seven levels of ANGER, but NARCISSISTIC RAGE goes from 0-7 in an instant.

The name actually comes from the Greek mythological[16] character Narcissus, who rejected love from others and fell in love with his own reflection in the water (see ECHOISM).

The unmet needs of the child meant they were unable to master critical emotional development. I discovered many years ago, you could understand the age that their TRAUMA happened, in certain situations they reverted to a child; if you think back you may recall that age; when they were threatened or they perceived danger, you may have noticed they walked or talked in a childish way.

Narcissism is a personality disorder which is diagnosed by a mental health professional. The NARCISSIST can't take RESPONSIBILITY for their actions. If you have been DISCARDED by one, it is likely you took the BLAME for the breakdown of the relationship so it is unlikely that they would agree to an appointment for a diagnosis.

I remember an old boss of mine being shocked that one of my clients was taking RESPONSIBILITY for a mistake one of his employees had made, which cost their company financially. He really couldn't understand why my client would do that. I tried to explain that a good manager takes RESPONSIBILITY for the actions of their staff when delegating projects. Ultimately it is their RESPONSIBILITY for the completion of the project.

A healthy person can see they have made a mistake and they try and correct that mistake or hold their hands up and say "yes, I'm sorry". They don't do everything in their POWER to prove there is nothing wrong with them, putting the BLAME on another person.

I refer to the NARCISSIST, SOCIOPATH AND PSYCHOPATH as EMOTIONAL ABUSERS or TOXIC people, they are much higher up on that NARCISSISTIC scale, but it is quite rare that one would get help.

Under the label of NARCISSIST, you will find different types:

Overt NARCISSIST • This is probably the type that jumps to mind. The grandiose sense of importance where the world revolves around them.

Covert NARCISSIST • They are as self-absorbed and as destructive in relationships as the overt, but they just aren't as loud and obvious.

Cerebral NARCISSIST • These are the know-it-alls, who use their intellect, or knowledge to secure their SUPPLY.

Somatic NARCISSIST • They flaunt their conquests and parade their possessions, or show off their muscles.

Inverted NARCISSISTS • They rely on other people for their emotional gratification, they have the tendency to put other people first, looking for relationships that make them feel validated or needed.

In a NARCISSIST'S mind, any attention is better than no attention. This means they are happy even if it is negative attention; in fact, they often find it more enjoyable, because if they can upset you, it means you still have deep EMOTIONS invested in them and the relationship.

Some of the techniques used to BOND you were changing your view of friends and family. As the NARCISSIST took over your life they made up stories and you began to see the ABUSER as the only person you could trust.

N is for NARCISSISTIC FLEAS • This is the term used[22] to describe a person who has been in a relationship with an EMOTIONALLY ABUSIVE or TOXIC person and displays similar behaviour.

If you were in a relationship with an EMOTIONALLY ABUSIVE or TOXIC person you were TRAUMA BONDED and you may have started to view the people and the world differently.

If you were brought up in this environment you may believe that MANIPULATIVE behaviour is normal. In CHILDREN ARE SPONGES I explain how we learn and take on our primary caregivers beliefs.

You may have been the SCAPEGOAT in your family or you may have experienced TRIANGULATION and you used this or other techniques. As you started to break away from your tribe you may have noticed that other people did not behave in this way or you didn't feel comfortable using them. As children we are all naturally NARCISSISTIC, but as we grow and mature we become aware of our environment and the people around us; we become sensitive to others feelings and their emotions and we understand the consequences of our actions.

As a result you may have Self-Parented yourself or you are now learning this is MANIPULATIVE behaviour.

You may have tried MIRRORING back the behaviour of the ABUSER as a defence mechanism, or as a way to give them "a taste of their own medicine".

In my experience acting like a NARCISSIST with the NARCISSIST doesn't have the same effect. They are usually completely unaffected, they are getting SUPPLY in the form of negative attention or they enjoy watching you try to use it. Your attention is on them and their needs, you might be showing them the pain you are in, validating them and showing them how much Power they still have over you.

N is for NARCISSISTIC INJURY • This is the term used to describe a threat, the NARCISSISTS perceives to their "false-self".

This INJURY is crushing for the ABUSER; it is seen as a serious criticism, total rejection or a threat to their very existence. Their response is swift, intense and out of proportion in the form of NARCISSISTIC RAGE.

N is for NARCISSISTIC RAGE • This is a reaction to NARCISSISTIC INJURY, which is a perceived threat to their SELF-ESTEEM or self-worth. There are seven levels of ANGER, but NARCISSISTIC RAGE goes from 0-7 in an instant.

There are two types of RAGE: explosive and passive-aggressive. Explosive RAGES are aggressive outbursts, which may be verbal or physical. With passive-aggressive RAGES, the NARCISSIST withdraws into sulky SILENT TREATMENT as a means of punishment. This RAGE is usually the result of childhood trauma, or an ABANDONMENT WOUND. The unmet needs of the child meant they were unable to master critical emotional development.

To understand the age that this TRAUMA happened, recall the age they reverted to when they perceived danger; the way they behaved in certain situations, you might have seen them behave like a 4 year old or a 6 year old. It might have been the way they moved or the language they used.

A word of caution: DO NOT EXCUSE THEIR BEHAVIOUR, understanding why they behave in the way they do does not make it OK! There are a lot of people who could say they had traumatic childhoods (and you could be one of them) that do not go round MANIPULATING people, hurting people or LYING to people.

N is for NARCISSISTIC SUPPLY • The term used to describe the constant attention that the NARCISSIST needs.

This will be from anyone who can provide attention, good or bad. You may have been DISCARDED if they had a New Source of SUPPLY (see REPLACEMENT and FINAL DISCARD).

NARCISSISTIC SUPPLY can come from work colleagues, friends, family members, the person next to them on the train or whoever serves them at the supermarket.

When you come out of an EMOTIONALLY ABUSIVE relationship, it is important you stop providing them with NARCISSISTIC SUPPLY. You can do this by going NO CONTACT, if for any reason you can't do this, then GREY ROCK is a solution.

N is for NO CONTACT • This is a tool you can use to protect yourself and your energy. This means cutting off all forms of communication with a person, to protect yourself from recurring trauma, allowing you to heal from the relationship.

This means deleting them from all social media, as well as blocking emails and phone contact.

This also means **you** don't look at their social media profiles, and if you find their FLYING MONKEYS on yours, block them as well!

I remember waking up one morning and seeing someone had liked a photo of mine two and a half years after we had separated. I had been stubborn up to that point claiming that I didn't have anything to hide, but that was the turning point and I blocked my accounts. A few months later I received an email and I blocked those too.

I have spoken to so many people who years later are still TRIGGERED receiving messages and emails. If you don't need to be in contact with them block and delete them.

If you have children together going NO CONTACT might be difficult. Explore any way you can to limit the contact you have with the ABUSER and try using GREY ROCK. Perhaps you could find someone who could help you with visitation or find a safe space to hand over your children.

Do you have anyone who can help you negotiate with them?

Be careful with mediation, they play the VICTIM so well, you may find yourself being portrayed in a bad light and the mediators siding with them. If you find yourself in this situation, keep reminding the mediators that **the focus should be on the children**. If you can, find people who understand what you have experienced they won't get drawn in.

O
is for...
reviveyoursoul.co.uk

And one day she discovered that she was fierce, and strong, and full of fire, and that not even she could hold herself back because her passion burned brighter than her fears.

Mark Anthony

O is for

O is for OBJECTIFICATION • This term is used to describe how an ABUSIVE or TOXIC person views and treats another.

If you experienced OBJECTIFICATION, you were not seen as person who had rights: you were seen as an OBJECT belonging to the ABUSER. You may have been denied the right to make decisions for yourself. You may not be addressed or introduced as a person.

OBJECTIFICATION causes you to lose your self-worth.

In families, it might be that a parent sees their child as an OBJECT encouraging the child to pursue activities that then gain them attention (see GOLDEN CHILD), having no regard for the child, or their feelings. They can then brag to their friends and family, or anyone that will listen about what their amazing child has done (this is different from being proud of a person's achievements). The ABUSER parent uses the child as a way of claiming the attention for themselves, they don't feel EMPATHY or have emotions so they don't feel proud, they get SUPPLY.

OBJECTIFICATION can continue after the relationship is over, with the ABUSER failing to relinquish CONTROL. It might be difficult to divorce the ABUSER or they still have

CONTROL in the way of finances. It can be particularly hard if you DISCARDED them.

O is for OXYTOCIN • During the LOVE BOMBING stage you received a lot of OXYTOCIN, which is a BONDING hormone. It is also known as the cuddle hormone or the love hormone, as it is released when people BOND socially, it can also be released when playing with a pet.

It plays a huge role during pregnancy, birth and breastfeeding. The release of OXYTOCIN starts labour and causes the contractions, it softens the neck of the cervix and then helps the uterus contract after birth. When the baby suckles at the breast, the stimulation releases OXYTOCIN promoting mother-child BONDING.

OXYTOCIN eases stress and creates feelings of calm and closeness. In a love relationship, your brain releases OXYTOCIN during physical contact, cuddling or sex; it is released when someone shows they trust you, and sometimes even simply by just talking.

Strong BONDS were created early on in the relationship, so when they started to DEVALUE you, it caused you great pain and confusion. If your reaction was disproportionate to the ending of the relationship, this could be an indication you were TRAUMA BONDED.

When the relationship ended, the BOND was so strong and the withdrawal was so painful, that you probably looked for ways of getting the relationship back to where you were at the beginning of the relationship; you felt secure there, you were receiving a lot of OXYTOCIN. And now you are addicted to the feeling it gives you.

But OXYTOCIN is two-faced[7]: as well as creating BONDS researchers have discovered it strengthens bad memories and can increase FEAR and anxiety. The hormone strengthens social memory in one specific region of the brain (the lateral septum) that intensifies the memory. If you experience a negative or stressful event or situation, OXYTOCIN activates that part of your brain. It intensifies the memory which can later lead to stressful TRIGGERS and reliving the emotions of the ORIGINAL WOUND through other experiences.

For example, let's say as a child you were lost in a large crowd, you didn't know where your parents or caregivers were, you felt anxious and ABANDONED, this is your ORIGINAL WOUND. Later you experience an event that creates the same feelings (this is the TRIGGER), and you then experience the same emotions and feelings from the ORIGINAL event. You may not recall the event as you are dealing with what is happening in your life, with this new situation. However you may find the way you deal with it is similar to the age from your ORIGINAL WOUND.

This is why I describe the ORIGINAL WOUND like a verruca; you need to get it all out otherwise it keeps coming back.

P
is for...
reviveyoursoul.co.uk

Grief can be the garden of compassion. If you keep your heart open through everything, your pain can become your greatest ally in your life's search for love and wisdom.

Rumi

P is for

P is for POWER and CONTROL • I use this term a lot throughout this book and my writing.

This is the MANIPULATION of one person over another. The EMOTIONAL ABUSER or TOXIC person is a MASTER of MANIPULATION, they use words and actions to deceive, COERCE, seduce, and mislead to gain POWER and CONTROL over everyone in their life. They are very insecure people, with their biggest FEAR being ABANDONMENT, and to ensure they will not be ABANDONED they need to CONTROL everyone and everything in their life.

P is for PSYCHOPATH • PSYCHOPATHS are unable to form EMOTIONAL attachments, or feel EMPATHY for others. They can be very charming, however they are MANIPULATIVE and can gain the trust of people easily. Although they don't feel emotion, they've learnt to mimic them, and can appear normal to most people.

Often PSYCHOPATHS are educated, have jobs and some have families, whilst others have long-term relationships, and some have both.

Contrary to common belief not all PSYCHOPATHS are Killers, but they are **Con-Artists**, and due to their calm and charismatic natures, anything they do is carefully planned in detail.

P is for PATHOLOGICAL LYING • Research has shown we all lie in one form or another, but this form of LYING is more calculated and harming. You may have told a lie to protect someone's feelings, perhaps about what they were wearing or a new hairstyle.

PATHOLOGICAL LYING is where someone lies to gain CONTROL over another person, and this is why relationships are games to them. They used LYING as a MASK during the IDEALISATION stage, presenting a false image of themselves. They MIRRORED you to become the person they believed you were looking for. They may have told you half-truths, or their words may have contained a sprinkling of truth, it helped make their stories sound believable and it helped them remember what they had told different people so they don't trip up.

P is for PROJECTING • This a tactic used to PROJECT their unhealed parts.

Most people are able to accept they might be wrong in a situation, or recognise something they said may have unintentionally hurt someone's feelings, and they are able to take RESPONSIBILITY for their actions.

However, EMOTIONAL ABUSERS or TOXIC People are unable to do this, instead, they PROJECTED all their broken and unhealed parts onto you.

They put themselves in a position of Power in your life which left you feeling vulnerable, terrified of ABANDONMENT and of being rejected, which was exactly how they felt.

PLEASE remember you are only RESPONSIBLE for your healing, not theirs!

Q
is for...
reviveyoursoul.co.uk

There is a sacredness in tears. They are not the mark of weakness, but of power. They speak more eloquently than ten thousand tongues. They are the messengers of overwhelming grief, of deep contrition, and of unspeakable love.

Washington Irving

Q is for

Q is for QUESTIONING • All the "what if's" and "maybe's"...

QUESTIONING the relationship: "was it real?"

And a really painful one, "did they really love me?"

Even more painful for me was the realisation that they didn't.

You may go back over the relationship step-by-step and QUESTION "what if" you had said something different or "what if" you hadn't said something.

Then you may go over the maybes: maybe if you had done something differently, would you be here? Maybe if you hadn't done something it would be different.

Eventually, you will realise that you couldn't have done anything differently. If you had, you would have been giving even more of your Soul away. The relationship may have lasted a little longer, but it was always going to end.

R
is for...
reviveyoursoul.co.uk

Remember, if you ever need a helping hand, it's at the end of your arm, as you get older, remember you have another hand: The first is to help yourself, the second is to help others.

Audrey Hepburn

R is for

R is for RAGING • RAGES threaten the security or safety of another individual and violate their personal BOUNDARIES (see NARCISSISTIC RAGE).

R is for RED FLAGS • A RED FLAG is a metaphor for something signalling a problem. RED FLAGS are used in motor racing to stop a race when there is danger. In the book *The Railway Children*[23], Roberta tore her red bloomers to make a RED FLAG, warning the train driver of danger. If you are a driver, signs with red backgrounds warn you to stop.

RED FLAGS are markers for concern. You have an ancient inbuilt warning system in your body; that GUT FEELING that tells you, you should be doing something, calling someone or perhaps you have a feeling you should go somewhere.

In other situations, you may feel that something isn't right or maybe a person is making you feel odd, this is your INTUITION.

During the IDEALISATION and DEVALUING stage, these feelings were turned off as you overlooked one RED FLAG after another.

If you did QUESTION their behaviour you were met with insincere apologies, or PROJECTION. You were the one who was insecure or had been treated badly in the past and this was why you felt this way, it wasn't their behaviour TRIGGERING you. If you had solid evidence of their behaviour they may have told you how sorry they were and they would never do it again.

Of course, they repeated this behaviour, as you had forgiven them and set another challenge for them because this was a game; how far could they push you before you would break.

R is for REPLACEMENT · You were REPLACED, they might have been secured before you were DISCARDED. The REPLACEMENT will experience the same treatment as you did, the empty promises and the planning of the FAKE FUTURE. They have REPLACED you and are now the only person who has ever really understood them.

This can be really painful, particularly if you are going through withdrawal symptoms, or it could be the CLOSURE you needed, after being fed lies making you feel CRAZY you then see them parading their new SUPPLY around.

You might feel the need to reach out to your REPLACEMENT and let them know exactly what they are getting themselves into, PLEASE DON'T!

Think back to the beginning of your relationship; if someone had approached you and tried to warn you, would you have listened? Or would you have ignored them believing they were a CRAZY eX?

R is for RESPONSIBILITY • (it's blank because they can't take any).

But YOU can take RESPONSIBILITY for your own life and your own healing.

You can use the techniques of NO CONTACT or GREY ROCK to protect yourself, or remove yourself from a situation, perhaps when a conversation gets heated, or is going round and round without a conclusion (see CIRCULAR CONVERSATIONS).

Give yourself time to clarify your thoughts. Explain that you need to process them and your feelings, take RESPONSIBILITY, "I need time to...", "I am feeling...", "I feel it would be better to discuss this..."

Understand and heal your ORIGINAL WOUND, find the root cause of the trigger and heal it.

S
is for...
reviveyoursoul.co.uk

Wherever you are, be there totally. If you find you're here and now intolerable and it makes you unhappy, you have three options: remove yourself from the situation, change it, or accept it totally. If you want to take responsibility for your life, you must choose one of those three options, and you must choose now. Then accept the consequences.

Eckhart Tolle

S is for

S is for SCAPEGOATING • The singling out of a person to take the BLAME for the wrongdoings or mistakes of another person is known as SCAPEGOATING[24].

It might be that the feelings of the ABUSER were not balanced, and they allowed how they felt about themselves to get in the way of the facts.

It could be that a parent singles out and punishes one child for the wrongdoings of their siblings.

Or it could be a teacher who allows their feelings towards a child to get in the way of the help or marks they give to that child, favouring other children in their care.

It might be a manager who singles out an employee for the more mundane work, and favours another employee.

SCAPEGOATING involves punishments rather than rewards and is based around judgement, it can bring up feelings of SHAME, ABANDONMENT and GUILT.

S is for SEXUAL COERCION • SEXUAL COERCION is unwanted sexual activity, where a person is pressured, tricked, threatened, or forced in a **non-physical** way.

The definition of COERCION is the action or practice of persuading someone to do something by using force or threats. Where as rape[25] is when a person intentionally penetrates another's vagina, anus or mouth with a penis, without the other person's consent. sexual assault[25] by penetration is when a person penetrates another person's vagina or anus with any part of the body other than a penis, or by using an OBJECT, without the person's consent.

SEXUAL COERCION is when a partner feels obliged or forced to perform a sexual act in a relationship.

You may have lived in FEAR that if you didn't do what the ABUSER wanted, there would be consequences or loss of the relationship. During the IDEALISATION and DEVALUATION stage the ABUSER used techniques to put more importance on the relationship than yourself.

They may have used TRIANGULATION, or been caught having an affair and used this to COERCE you into performing certain sexual acts that you did not want to participate in, or were not comfortable with.

S is for SHAMING • SHAME is a painful emotion caused by the belief that you are inferior, or unworthy.

SHAMING is a technique used to divert attention away from the ABUSER'S own bad behaviour and PROJECTING that onto you.

This was used to make you believe you were the problem in order for them to stay in CONTROL. It was also a way of hiding their insecurities and pushing the attention onto you, when they themselves are experiencing SHAME.

S is for SILENT TREATMENT • A passive-aggressive form of EMOTIONAL ABUSE. It is a way of showing displeasure, or disapproval.

This was a tool used to punish you and to bring up feelings of FEAR and guilt. They may have chosen not to hear you, or walked away when you were talking. They intentionally withheld attention from you to prove the Power and CONTROL they had over you. SILENT TREATMENT is CONDITIONAL LOVE, which was used to MANIPULATE you.

You may have experienced this form of punishment from a parent or caregiver and you may believed this is acceptable behaviour (see NARCISSISTIC FLEAS).

As children we lived in a theta state (see CHILDREN ARE SPONGES) up until the age of seven or eight and we took on the beliefs of our family unit, our tribe, which has possibly been passed down through the generations.

You may need to remove yourself from a situation, perhaps when a conversation gets heated, or it is going round and round with no conclusion or has been resurrected again (see CIRCULAR CONVERSATIONS), or you may need time to clarify your thoughts, this is different from the SILENT TREATMENT, you are doing this to protect yourself, not to MANIPULATE another person or a situation.

S is for SMEAR CAMPAIGN • The definition of a SMEAR CAMPAIGN is "a plan to discredit a public figure by making false accusations". Take out the public figure and REPLACE it with your name.

SMEAR CAMPAIGNS are designed to ensure the ABUSER looks like the VICTIM. They created stories about the terrible things you had allegedly said or done. They wanted to punish you and, as they can't take RESPONSIBILITY; you were the problem. This may have started before the FINAL DISCARD. The SMEAR CAMPAIGN could have involved mutual friends, members of your family or even your children.

You may have asked yourself "why would someone do that?" and the simple reason was to create a situation where they would get more attention and they didn't have to take the RESPONSIBILITY for their behaviour.

If you think back to the IDEALISATION stage of your relationship, they were telling you that you were the only person who has ever fully understood them, they were telling you stories about their eXes. This was a SMEAR CAMPAIGN, they were doing the same then, but at the time you were being drugged up with OXYTOCIN and DOPAMINE. You probably saw how they treated other people, but believed they would never do that to you.

They are now telling similar stories about you; the awful way they were spoken to, the awful way they were treated and they may claim you are bipolar or have an addiction.

This behaviour excites them, it gives them a sense of Power and it gives them the SUPPLY they so desperately need.

As you experienced the EMOTIONAL pain, trying to understand what happened, they took it further and told everyone what was wrong with you, and you may have experienced feelings of ABANDONMENT, SHAME and guilt.

Once you start to understand what happened to you, you may want to tell everyone who they really are, you will want to UNMASK them, but I urge you not to!

The CRAZY eX they told you about, you are going join that club: don't give them the fuel.

S is for SOCIOPATH • The term SOCIOPATH is used to describe a person who lacks or has a weak conscience; whereas the PSYCHOPATH has no conscience whatsoever.

The SOCIOPATH is able to socialise and takes their cues from other people around them; they show signs of caring, sincerity, and trustworthiness, but like the NARCISSIST and PSYCHOPATH they are also MANIPULATIVE, often LIE and they act recklessly.

They know their behaviour is wrong and they may feel some guilt or remorse, but that doesn't stop them. Like the NARCISSIST and PSYCHOPATH, they lack EMPATHY and are prone to emotional outbursts, including fits of RAGE.

S is for SOULMATES • This reference is to MANUFACTURED SOULMATES. During the IDEALISATION stage, they told you, and anyone who would listen how amazing you were, and how you were meant to be together, that you were SOULMATES!

A SOUL MATE connection is a deep profound connection with another person: your connection was MANUFACTURED by the ABUSER.

They love the idea of being a romantic; they love the attention it gives them.

They were creating a BOND; the more they talked about it, the more you started to believe them.

You had so much in common. You had mapped out your FAKE FUTURE together! They had put on a MASK and were playing the person of your dreams. You were the only person that had really understood who they were and their needs.

You might have experienced an instant connection with them, they felt very familiar; you may have felt that you had known them all your life.

If this was your experience it is likely what you recognised was a similar relationship to one you may have had before or with a parent or caregiver. You were recognising a pattern of behaviour that felt familiar to you.

S is for STOCKHOLM SYNDROME • When a hostage, kidnap VICTIM or ABUSE VICTIM develops a sense of loyalty and attaches to their captor or ABUSER, it is known as the STOCKHOLM SYNDROME[26].

The term "STOCKHOLM SYNDROME" was coined by Swedish psychiatrist and criminologist Nils Bejerot. He was involved in a case following a bank robbery that went wrong in Stockholm on 23 August 1973. The robber Jan-Erik Olsson held four bank employees hostage for six days. As part of his negotiations with the police, Olsson's friend Clark Olofsson was allowed to enter the bank. The two then BONDED with the hostages who in turn acted to protect their captors, despite being repeatedly threatened by them.

During the IDEALISATION stage, a lot of care and attention was given to securing your relationship, and it was tested many times, to ensure you were HOOKED; and that your focus was on protecting the relationship, not yourself. The attention you received during that time you may never have experienced before, so when the DEVALUATION started it confused you, you didn't understand how this amazing person could change at the flick of a switch. COGNITIVE DISSONANCE plays a part in this as well, along with our internal survival instincts (see THE FOUR F's).

Instead of seeing the ABUSE as a threat, you JUSTIFIED it. After all, how could someone who worshipped the ground you walked on, your SOULMATE, who you had so much in common with and shared the same hopes and dreams, be an ABUSER?

S is for SUICIDAL IDEATION • The pain of not wanting to be alive is SUICIDAL IDEATION. Pete Walker[14] describes it as common phenomenon in C-PTSD particularly during intense or prolonged flashbacks. It is fantasising or thinking about wanting to die.

Perhaps you wake up in the morning realising you are still alive and wondering how you are going get through another day. You may have thoughts wishing you weren't alive anymore, believing there is nothing to live for. You are now left wondering how you will live without them and what there is to live for.

You might have thoughts of having an accident, stepping out in front of a car or going to sleep and never waking up again. This is passive suicidality which is not a serious intent to kill yourself.

Active suicidality is when a person is actively proceeding in the direction of taking their life. This is less common but if you are considering actively ending your life, please seek help. The Samaritans operate a 24 hour helpline in the UK call 116 123 or in the US call 1-800-273-8255.

S is for SUPPLY • Think of an electric car, for it to work it needs to be plugged into an energy source, once fully charged you can unplug it and drive off. Or a rechargeable vacuum cleaner: when it starts to lose POWER you plug it back in and charge it. Like the car or vacuum the EMOTIONAL ABUSER needs a source of SUPPLY for them to function.

SUPPLY to the EMOTIONAL ABUSER is attention, and they surround themselves with people who can provide it to them. Their main source of SUPPLY will be from their main partner and a secondary source of SUPPLY may come from children, work colleagues and family members or it may come from an affair (see Short Relationships).

They plug into people and once they have taken everything they need they then move on, topping up as they move throughout their day. They don't really care where it comes from as long as the focus is on them.

If you have been DISCARDED by an EMOTIONAL ABUSER it is likely the SUPPLY you were providing was getting weaker as they had broken down your BOUNDARIES and MANIPULATED you to a point you could barely function, draining you EMOTIONALLY, Mentally, Physically, Spiritually and it was possible you were no longer able to support them financially.

They caused chaos in your life; they then walked away without a backward glance and left you to pick up the pieces, whilst they played the VICTIM, which is another source of SUPPLY for them.

They might have started to lay the groundwork before their departure, testing the water, checking how people will perceive them, making up stories and starting their SMEAR CAMPAIGN.

They are empty inside and they need the attention of others to function. They don't really care if it is positive or negative, or where it comes from. They are not able to validate themselves, so they look outside themselves for this.

They have no identity, and they don't really like who they are, so they create new personalities, and they actually believe these characters are an extension of themselves. They believed the lies they told you, and they have an innate ability to believe the words that come out of their own mouths. These untruths are now the truth.

T
is for...
reviveyoursoul.co.uk

Holding on to anger is like grasping a hot coal with the intent of throwing it at someone else; you are the one who gets burned.

Buddha

T is for

T is for TOXIC • The definition of TOXIC is poisonous relating to, or caused by poison. You were probably taught at a young age not to touch a TOXIC substance, and shown the label indicating the contents of the bottle or packet were poisonous; the skull and crossbones on a yellow background.

People can also be TOXIC and so can relationships.

The TOXIC person might be the friend, family member or partner who talks at you, rather than have a conversation with you. They might be the person who wants to take over your life, everything you do, think and say. Not allowing you to have an opinion or allow you to give your view.

They might be an energy vampire, who manages to drain the life out of everyone in the room. Or they might be the person that constantly needs your support with tea and sympathy, but they are not interested in your views or in any advice you have to offer. They actually don't want to want to fix the problem, like a butterfly going from flower to flower they move to the next person with the same problem.

Or you may have a JEALOUS person in your life. They can't be happy for anyone else as they have such LOW SELF-ESTEEM. Their JEALOUSY comes across in the judgement and criticism of others. Or there might be the TOXIC person who LIES, or exaggerates the facts, you find your intuition is telling you that what they are saying isn't exactly true.

You may not have noticed their behaviour before, but as you are healing yourself you find you dread seeing certain people.

You may recognise them in your life as friends, family members or colleagues.

You might start to realise they don't respect you, or your opinions. You might see a pattern in your relationship with them, perhaps you are constantly having to save someone or fix their problems, you may feel angry, sad or depressed when you are around them and you start to feel them draining your energy or you are afraid of them.

You might have noticed they go missing when you need help or advice with a problem and then reappear when you have recovered enough to listen and support them again. Or you might find a VULTURE appear.

T is for TRAUMA BONDING • We develop BONDS for survival in childhood, usually with our caregiver, who is the foundation of attachment. When our safety is threatened in some way, we turn to them for support and protection.

TRAUMA BONDING is one of the reasons it is so hard to heal from TOXIC and EMOTIONALLY ABUSIVE relationships. The damage caused puts you into a state of confusion as you had no idea the ABUSE was taking place.

The term was developed by Patrick Carnes[27] who describes it as "The misuse of fear, excitement, sexual feelings, and sexual physiology to entangle another person"[28].

BONDING happens in all relationships, but this type of BONDING was one-sided, and this is why it was so easy for them to walk away, as they didn't BOND to you.

When our safety is threatened in some way, we turn to our tribe for support and protection and these BONDS can be created within hours.

BONDING is a process that makes people more important to each other, we develop BONDS for survival, and it is the foundation of attachment.

This is why team building exercises use scenarios and techniques that help instil trust in each other, BONDS are made during activities that are unique to the individuals.

People who have experienced a traumatic situation together always have a BOND of survival.

BONDING is a very strong connection, and it strengthens when we spend time with someone, make love, and when we have children together.

TRAUMA BONDING is used by the EMOTIONAL ABUSER or TOXIC person to enable them to gain POWER and CONTROL over you.

During the IDEALISATION stage, they positioned themselves as the caregiver, showering you with attention, gifts, meals, days out, MANUFACTURING a love you may never have experienced before.

They then started DEVALUING you, with slight put-downs and TRIANGULATION, or GASLIGHTING. You may have rationalised their behaviour, believing they cared about you, creating even more BONDING. This was the reason you were so connected to them, and when the relationship ended, you wondered how you would survive.

TRAUMA BONDING made it hard to enforce BOUNDARIES, which was why it was so painful to stay away from them.

After getting you addicted to OXYTOCIN and DOPAMINE through the LOVE BOMBING, they started to introduce situations that released stress hormones (see THE FOUR F's). This was done with the slight put-downs and by creating drama, MANUFACTURING these emotions.

When they threatened your safety through their bad behaviour, you turned to them, for help and protection. You rationalised their behaviour, believing they cared about you, this created further BONDING, which was the reason you felt so connected to them. When the relationship finished, your stress levels were so high, you experienced FEAR and couldn't imagine your life without them.

They on the other hand played the VICTIM, and you very likely believed this was all your fault and the pain you now feel, runs deep into your Soul.

T is for TRIANGULATION • Another tool they love to use for MANIPULATION is TRIANGULATION. These insecure people used it to gain MANUFACTURED EMOTIONS of JEALOUSY and insecurity from you.

TRIANGULATION is used for NARCISSISTIC SUPPLY. When they surrounded themselves with, or talked about members of the opposite sex, friends, colleagues, former lovers (who they initially told you awful stories about), and future lovers, they were creating the illusion of popularity. TRIANGULATION was used to create JEALOUSY and tension. This was a very specific pattern used during the DEVALUATION stage and maybe a sprinkling in the IDEALISATION stage, to gain CONTROL.

They used TRIANGULATION on a regular basis to give the illusion they were in high demand, keeping you on your toes; making sure you were aware of what you needed to do to keep in their inner circle as they secured you further into the relationship. They used it to ensure you were more invested in the relationship than you were in yourself.

You were aware of what happened in their other relationships, and you knew about their CRAZY eXes. You knew what went wrong in those relationships, but you were so HOOKED up to the attention you received, you didn't want to let go of that drug.

This was a game; you didn't have the rules. They enjoy turning people against each other and they got an even bigger kick when it was about them.

This also happens in families, and you may have experienced it growing up, children were pitted against each other (see GOLDEN CHILD V SCAPEGOAT).

You may have experienced GASLIGHTING, which made you QUESTION yourself as they claimed that you were JEALOUS; are you a JEALOUS person? They might have brought up your past relationships and telling you this was all your fault because you had trust issues.

They might have told you what other people thought of you; this was to make you feel insecure.

You may have been kept away from the people they used to TRIANGULATE you; partly because they couldn't risk you talking to each other, and realising they hadn't said, done or been...(fill in the blank). They couldn't risk you discovering the truth, but also it created JEALOUSY, wondering why you were not being included.

By MANUFACTURING these situations, your emotions were heightened, you experienced JEALOUSY, neediness, RAGE, anxiety, doubt and insecurity. These were carefully MANUFACTURED, you may have QUESTIONED their fidelity. A normal person would want to ensure you felt secure in your relationship, they wouldn't create FEAR in you.

And, of course, you were the CRAZY one, just like Amy, Beth and Cherie (insert name): the CRAZY eX before you.

T is for TRIBE • The definition of a TRIBE is a social division in a traditional society consisting of families or communities linked by social, economic, religious, or blood ties, with a common culture and dialect, typically having a recognised leader.

When you hear the word TRIBE you may think of the Indigenous tribes from Australia or Native Americans, or TRIBES from Africa.

Your TRIBE is your support network. The group of people who may, or may not, be related by blood. They are the people who have your back. They are the people who understand who you are. They are the people only want the best for you, who won't hold you back from attaining your goals and dreams.

T is for TRIGGER • A TRIGGER can be anything that brings up a memory - a smell or a sight or a sound.

A TRIGGER could also be hearing a name, getting a text message or an email and when they are TRAUMA-based they send the body into FIGHT, FLIGHT, FAWN or FREEZE (The FOUR F's) and you may experience FEAR, SHAME or guilt.

Memories may come up for you, which TRIGGER EMOTIONAL FLASHBACKS.

This is one of the reasons you need to go NO CONTACT. Your body needs the chance to calm down with all the cortisol that has been rushing through it. (see C-PTSD).

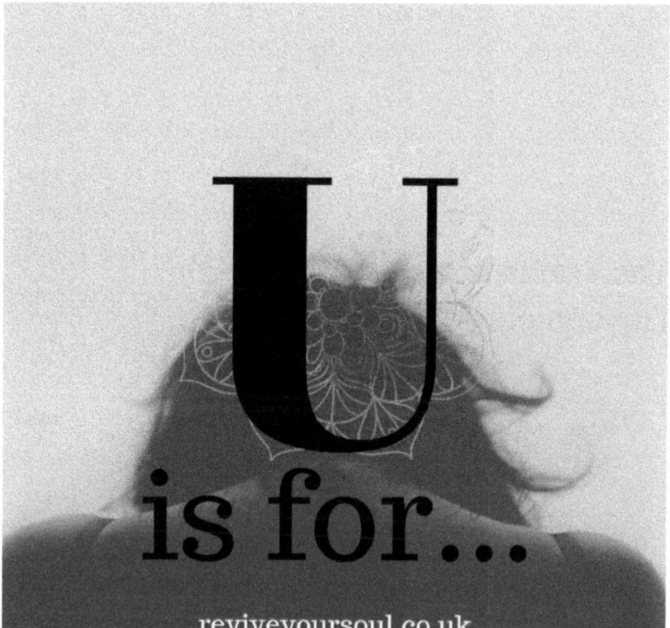
U
is for...
reviveyoursoul.co.uk

The wound is the place where the
Light enters you.

Rumi

U is for

U is for MANUFACTURED UNDYING LOVE • I added this one, I didn't hear it or read about it when I was trying to understand what happened to me.

However, it is one of the MANIPULATION tools used to HOOVER you back up. I didn't realise it was HOOVERING at the time, I heard statements "you shouldn't be doing this on your own" and "we are SOULMATES and we should be together" and "I should be there with you helping you get through this".

When I said "OK, let's give it another try", I was met with a different story. "I'm so busy" and "I have so many people who rely on me" and "If we are to have a future together..." followed by a list of demands.

This wasn't UNDYING LOVE this was about POWER and CONTROL. This was MANUFACTURED to make sure I was still invested in the relationship enough to do anything asked of me. This was MANUFACTURED for SUPPLY.

During the DISCARD stages (and I use the plural because there are many of them), you were sucked back in, you knew something wasn't right in your relationship, and you may have even QUESTIONED what was going on. You were told this was all your fault; they highlighted your insecurities, and then when they were ready, they HOOVERED you back up. Perhaps the ABUSER told you they were really sorry and promised they wouldn't do it again, or they hadn't realised how much you meant to them, and how important the relationship was to them until now.

I have often likened the CYCLE OF ABUSE to a fisherman. The fisherman casts out their line with the bait attached, waiting for the fish to bite. When they feel a tug on the line, they don't try to land the fish straight away, instead, they may create a little tension on the line but they wait. They allow the fish to swim away, giving it a false sense of security, but all the time the hook is in its mouth, and once they feel the fish has HOOKED, the fisherman starts to reel in the line and then they land it.

During the relationship you were programmed. Everything you experienced was everything you were looking for, and that is why it was so hard to let go. Just as the person standing at the slot machine finds it hard to walk away so did you, you had invested so much, even though you saw the RED FLAGS.

But it wasn't real, you told them who you were looking for.

All the QUESTIONS they asked at the beginning of the relationship, you believed, were because they were interested in you. However, their QUESTIONS were actually to understand what character they needed to create to hook you.

Like a writer who gets an idea for a book; they knew everything about the person they were creating.

And they loved this part of the game because they got so much attention from it. Every time they did something they were rewarded, "You did this for me?" "You were thinking of me... you are so thoughtful!" "Wow, you are so amazing and so kind"... And BOOM just like a puffer fish they explode with pride.

V
is for...
reviveyoursoul.co.uk

Our greatest glory is not in never falling,
but in rising every time we fall.

Confucius

V is for

V is for VICTIM • Definition • *A person harmed, injured, or killed as a result of a crime, accident, or other event or action. Synonyms • sufferer, the injured party, casualty, injured person, wounded person.*

You would think, coming out of an EMOTIONALLY ABUSIVE relationship, you would be the VICTIM, but the ABUSER claims they are. They lead you to believe you were the ABUSER, and during the DEVALUATION stage, you lost your SELF-ESTEEM.

When they were TRIANGULATING you, you began to believe you weren't good enough. You saw the RED FLAGS, but they made excuses, and you were so invested in the relationship, you forgot about yourself.

During the IDEALISATION stage, they discovered your insecurities, which they claimed were the same as theirs and later during a DISCARD or the FINAL DISCARD they used these against you.

You are left feeling that you are to BLAME for the ABUSE, and this is completely normal. You were conditioned and groomed to absorb all of the problems in the relationship. Once you understand the role you played, you are ready to heal.

V is for VULTURES • At the end of an EMOTIONALLY ABUSIVE relationship, you may experience extremes of emotions (see C-PTSD).

The people around you are usually quite shocked. You pretended to the outside world that everything was OK, perhaps better than OK, you MASKED what was really going on behind closed doors.

During the TRAUMA BONDING you handed over Power and CONTROL of your life, so when the relationship ends you very painfully experience FEAR. You were told how lucky you were to have them in your life; you were BONDED to them, you QUESTIONED your friendships and your relationships with your family; they had played MINDFUCKERY and you were left unable to function on your own.

When you finally found the courage to share your story you find people have disappeared, however others step forward. There are people who will happily listen to your story for hours on end, unfortunately, they may not be the people who are invested in your recovery.

VULTURES[21] at first seem kind and warm, they want to help fix you, and they are happy to listen to your problems.

You may realise over time they give you advice, but you find they also need constant praise and attention, and that they are not as invested in you as you believed they were. As you start to recover, they may challenge you because they really want you to stay trapped.

In the beginning, you do need to talk, nothing makes sense, you are so confused, you may also be experiencing symptoms of C-PTSD: once your body has started to calm down you need some deeper healing to ensure you don't do this again.

Find a tribe, you do need help understanding this was not your fault. If you can, find a professional therapist or recovery communities. Find people who understand what you have been through, and who are going to want you to heal and grow.

W
is for...
reviveyoursoul.co.uk

The human being is a self-propelled automaton entirely under the control of external influences. Wilful and predetermined though they appear, his actions are governed not from within, but from without. He is like a float tossed about by the waves of a turbulent sea.

Nikola Tesla

W is for

W is for WALKING ON EGGSHELLS • This term is used to describe the way you behaved around the ABUSIVE person, being very careful not to upset them and cause a NARCISSISTIC RAGE.

You tiptoed around a person or situation in order to protect yourself, your children, or those around you. You avoided saying or doing something to keep the peace, not wanting to wake up the monster.

W is for WORD SALAD • This is a form of communication[21] which doesn't make sense, it fails to progress the discussion in any way or where there is no outcome. This is done in various ways, it could be a combination of CIRCULAR CONVERSATIONS, PROJECTING and BLAME SHIFTING.

This was all done in an attempt to confuse you and gain CONTROL over the conversation and you!

These conversations didn't make sense, and when you tried to understand what was actually being said, they moved the conversation on in a different direction. They brought up your wrong doings as an attempt to cover up their behaviour, and they played the VICTIM.

If you tried to be part of the conversation (which is really one-sided so is more rhetorical) you were told to stop interrupting them. When they did allow you to speak, they talked over the top of you, confusing you further and you possibly ended up giving in wondering what happened, leaving them feeling POWERFUL.

X
is for...
reviveyoursoul.co.uk

If you tell the truth, you don't have to remember anything.

Mark Twain

X is for

X is for CRAZY eX • They talked about their eXes far more than any healthy individual should in a new relationship. During the IDEALISATION stage, they told you that you were the only person who had fully understood them: you were SOULMATES.

Once they secured you, they told you the stories about their CRAZY eX. They might have been subjected to bipolar or CRAZY MAKING behaviour during and after the relationship. They might have told you stories of their eX being bitter, JEALOUS or still in love with them, this may have been true. However, it is not normal for someone to have attracted so many CRAZY relationships and, with them being the common thread, is it possible they are the reason for the CRAZINESS?

Y
is for...
reviveyoursoul.co.uk

Always forgive your enemies; nothing annoys them so much.

Oscar Wilde

Y is for

Y is for whY? • All those QUESTIONS... Why did this happen to me? Why would they do that? Why am I so confused? Why have I taken the BLAME?

Why Why Why...

Why did this happen to you?

I like to think that there is a beautiful lesson to be learnt and a WOUND that is ready to be healed.

Why would they do that?

They love to play with people, it gives them a sense of POWER. It is also a MASK for the insecure person they really are. They SHAME people before they are SHAMED, they ABANDON people before they are ABANDONED, and they make people feel guilty to extract the SUPPLY they need. They feed off them like vampires, they sucked out your Soul like a DEMENTOR.

Why am I taking the BLAME?

Because you were told this was your fault and they can't take RESPONSIBILITY for anything. And they like to play the VICTIM. The ABUSER causes havoc everywhere they go, and they walk away leaving everyone else to clear up their mess. They TRAUMA BONDED you, and they

GASLIGHT you, leaving you so confused and believing you are the CRAZY one - when in reality, they are.

Z
is for...
reviveyoursoul.co.uk

I believe that everything happens for a reason. People change so that you can learn to let go, things go wrong so that you appreciate them when they're right, you believe lies so you eventually learn to trust no one but yourself, and sometimes good things fall apart so better things can fall together.

Marilyn Monroe

Z is for

Z is for craZy MAKING • (see COGNITIVE DISSONANCE) CRAZY MAKING in relationships is a dynamic used to make you QUESTION yourself and leaving you full of self-doubt, wondering if you might be going CRAZY.

It is a form of EMOTIONAL ABUSE involving mind games. It erodes your confidence, slowly allowing the other person to gain more Power and CONTROL over you and the relationship. You end up QUESTION your sanity and find yourself becoming more emotional, needy or dependent on the other person.

Do you still believe you did something wrong, and this was all your fault?

If you do, then think about it this way.

Everything else they told you was a lie - so why do you believe them about this?

The Dark Night of the Soul

The Dark Night of the Soul is a description of a process of inner healing; it might be for one night, it might be for several or it may go on for weeks, months and even years.

The Dark Night of the Soul[32] is the deepest darkest emotion; like being trapped in a cave and not knowing how you are going to find your way out.

It is a pain that runs so very deeply, moving through your heart and your Soul; any audible cries are more like an animal crying out in pain.

If you can, picture yourself, breaking out of a shell or a mould, you are shedding the chains that have bound you for so long.

So what is the "Dark Night of the Soul"?

Perhaps you have been experiencing this pain. The Dark Night of the Soul is described by Eckhart Tolle[28] as "a collapse of a perceived meaning in life...an eruption into your life of a deep sense of meaninglessness. The inner state in some cases is very close to what is conventionally called depression"

This process can occur at any point in your life, and some may never experience it.

The Dark Night of the Soul is a transitional period – a clearing out of the old to move on with the new.

If you have experienced the ABANDONMENT at the end of a TOXIC relationship, the Dark Night of the Soul has probably been TRIGGERED. It usually occurs after a major event happening in your life that takes you so deep to a point of QUESTIONING.

It has been described as a beautiful experience but perhaps it isn't until afterwards you can see that.

The beauty described is the reduction of the ego and the evolving of Self-Love!

When I think about the Dark Night of the Soul now, I think of it now as the process the caterpillar goes through to become a butterfly. It literally breaks down in to something unrecognisable and if you were to break the cocoon open a goo would seep out. The caterpillar uses enzymes to breakdown and reconstruct itself and the only thing that doesn't change is its DNA. And once it has emerged it rests; the wings of the butterfly are still wet and too delicate to fly.

It's now your time to move on... leave behind the old you and step forward.

If you can, picture an image of yourself, breaking out of a shell or a cast – shedding the chains that have bound you.

The next time you experience this emotion (and there are varying degrees of this), see yourself as a butterfly emerging and get ready to embrace the new world.

So, to summarise....

If their lips are moving, they're probably LYING.

If you feel something is wrong, then it probably is, despite them trying to make you believe this is your fault.

If you have caught them cheating, they will apologise and beg your forgiveness, telling you they will never do it again, but they will, they will just disguise it better.

If they keep promising to change, they won't, they will learn to disguise it better.

If you are wondering why they treat others the way they do, be ready to be treated the same way when you are no longer of use to them. They will be telling your REPLACEMENT they are the only person who has ever really understood them.

If you find they never take RESPONSIBILITY and always play the VICTIM, ask yourself who is the common denominator.

If it isn't tied down, it is theirs.

If you find your money is their money and their money is their own, this is COERCIVE CONTROL.

If their conversations confuse you, they are meant to, they are either bored or, they are distracting you from what is really going on.

If you find you are cancelling or rearranging your plans and that your friends are disappearing, you are being CONTROLLED.

A-Z

of Emotional Abuse

Support your Healing Journey

Dear Reader,

I want you to imagine standing in a swimming pool with a beach ball, how long can you hold that ball under the water?

The trauma that we experience throughout our lives are like beach balls, and we can only internalise them for so long before they appear wanting attention. This could be in the way of a friendship that is similar to one you have had before; a partner similar to one you have experienced before. Have you ever asked yourself "why does this keep happening me?"

The emotions that come up are like little bubbles. Holding onto them can cause illness in your body and your mind.

If this book has affected you in any way, please speak to someone, turn your pain into a positive experience.

You do not have to relive any of it, there are ways to release pain and trauma effectively, and this is how I help clients.

I have added a few ideas to help you release the trauma and I have included the Hawaiian Forgiveness Prayer, Ho'oponopono, to help with forgiveness.

Sending you loads of love,

Elizabeth Goddard

Writing the story....

The power of words is so, so healing. Use your story to understand what happened. With a pen and a notebook write it out by hand, which I believe is so powerful. It can be in any order, you can start at the beginning or in the middle, what memory is coming up for you?

Once you have written your story and then go back through this book and see if you can identify any of the terms used.

Were you Gaslighted?

Can you see the Cycle of Abuse?

Did you experience Alienation?

Were you Triangulated?

Connecting the Dots.

Make a list of all the people you know, past and present and see if you can see similar personality types, include people you have worked with and family members. You may have worked with some amazing people, but there may have been one person that made your life difficult.

When I did this, I realised one person was the real reason behind me leaving a job. They consistently undermined me after I was promoted over them twice. I could see how they had recruited their FLYING MONKEYS, and it was really healing.

Befriending Your PFF

When you come out of these types of relationships, the trauma runs deep, to the core of your being. You may still believe this is all your fault.

But I want you to think about this. The relationship was MANUFACTURED, and they told you a lot of untruths. Do you still agree with the voices in your head, reminding you, what an awful person you are?

Challenge the Personal Fault Finder[30]. Its job is to whisper in your ear reminding you of your faults; it spends time telling you you're going to fail, so not to start...

In this situation befriend the inner critic, the voice repeating what you have been told. We start by using a technique called befriending.

Think of your best friend. If you don't have one, think back to an old friend you had or a family member or teacher or work colleague, someone who really cared for your wellbeing.

When you hear a statement in your head, or feel the pain emanating from your Soul, ask yourself whose is this belief.

And then ask yourself these three questions:

Q1. Would my best friend agree with my views?

Q2. If not, what would they say about me?

Q3. Why would my friend see me differently?

If it helps write this down and see these emotions like the little bubbles that need releasing.

Ho'oponopono

I am sorry

Please forgive me

Thank you

I love you

Ho'oponopono[29] is a very ancient Hawaiian art of problem solving. It is a gift to be shared and practiced.

Morrnah Simeona is recognised for updating and bringing it forward. She was a healer from Hawaii and taught her updated version of *Ho'oponopono* throughout the United States, Asia and Europe.

Morrnah was a practitioner of Lomilomi massage and for 10 years owned and operated health spas at the Kahala Hilton and Royal Hawaiian hotels.

She felt it was difficult for the Western mind to get a grasp of a Higher Being because of traditional Western churches; and said "Western man has gone to the extremes with his intellectualism, it divides and keeps people separate. Man then becomes a destroyer because he manages and copes, rather than letting the perpetuating force of the Divinity flow through him for right action."[29]

Recognising the depth of dis-ease and pain which western civilisation needed healing she knew that *Ho'oponopono* could help.

Ho'oponopono means to make right or to rectify an error.

Traditionally the entire family would attend the healing, with a moderator present, each family member had a chance to ask for forgiveness from the others.

Knowing western communities and families were fragmented she began to develop a new form of *Ho'oponopono,* modifying the original process in 1976.

Her system is simple and can be used successfully by anyone.

The healing process includes one's Soul and the Divine. Morrnah has said,

We can appeal to Divinity who knows our personal blueprint, for healing of all thoughts and memories that are holding us back at this time...It is a matter of going beyond traditional means of accessing knowledge about ourselves.

We are the sum total of our experiences, which is to say that we are burdened by our pasts. When we experience stress or FEAR in our lives, if we would look carefully, we would find that the cause is actually a memory. It is the emotions which are tied to these memories which

affect us now. The subconscious associates an action or person in the present with something that happened in the past. When this occurs, emotions are activated and stress is produced.

"I'm sorry

Please forgive me

Thank you

I love you"

By saying these words over and over, a person is said to connect her/his own inner light with the light of Source. Over time patterns in the subconscious dissolve, and by forgiving the parts within that hold those patterns, the person's outer world regains balance and harmony.

Consider this...

Part of you fell in love with yourself!

They were MIRRORING all your amazing qualities within themselves; everything they are missing, the EMPATHY and caring for others.

Your inner beauty and your deep forgiving Soul! I believe these people are very insecure, and they are constantly needing validation. I don't know if they realise how much damage and hurt they cause, or if they in fact care. BUT I want to you realise you fell in LOVE with YOURSELF in a roundabout twisted way!

You are an amazing person!

I know you are hurting and have been for a long time, but NOW is the time to fall back in LOVE with you! The only person you are RESPONSIBLE for is yourself.

You may believe you can help them, after all, you may still believe you are the only one who has ever understood them fully, but you sadly can't.

They may agree to relationship counselling, but unless the counsellor has experience working with personality disordered people, they may believe the ABUSER'S stories, and you leave wondering what happened, and believing this is all your fault. After all, a professional is agreeing with them.

I was lucky enough to find someone who wanted to work separately and was able to highlight to me that I wasn't the person at fault. She did have her work cut out as I was so focused on trying to get the relationship back to where we had been at the beginning of the relationship, I was prepared - at all costs to my mental and emotional state - to take the BLAME for everything.

I was really lucky to work with another counsellor who would challenge me and explained to me what had been going on in the relationship.

For me, time and investment were non-negotiable.

To support your Healing Journey you can access 3 Meditations by visiting

https://www.reviveyoursoul.co.uk/a-z-emotional-abuse-meditations

password: A-ZMeditations

References

I have spent 1000s of hours watching YouTube videos and 1000s of hours reading books.

I have bought online courses and talked to many professionals.

The references in this book are from books, articles and articles I found are listed below.

1. Debbie Ford Dark Side of the Light Chasers: Reclaiming your power, creativity, brilliance, and dreams Publisher: Hodder Paperbacks (2 Aug. 2001) ISBN-10: 0340819057 ISBN-13: 978-0340819050

2. John Welwood Love and Awakening Discovering the Sacred Path of Intimate Relationship Publisher: HarperSanFrancisco (30 Sept. 1998) ISBN-10: 0060927976 ISBN-13: 978-0060927974

3. Ross Rosenburg The Human Magnet Syndrome: Why We Love People Who Hurt Us Premier Publishing & Media (9 July 2013) ISBN-10: 1936128314 ISBN-13: 978-1936128310

4. It causes so much damage Emotional Abuse and Brain Structural Damage https://www.selfgrowth.com/articles/emotional-abuse-and-brain-structural-damage

5. We are all a bunch of chemicals! BLOG 14th February 2017 Love, Actually: The science behind lust, attraction, and companionship Katherine Wu http://sitn.hms.harvard.edu/flash/2017/love-actually-science-behind-lust-attraction-companionship/

6. Triggers and #metoo The Guardian 15th January 2018 Emma Brockes#MeToo founder Tarana Burke: "You have to use your privilege to serve other people" https://www.theguardian.com/world/2018/jan/15/me-too-founder-tarana-burke-women-sexual-assault

7. Science Daily "Love hormone" is two-faced: Oxytocin strengthens bad memories and can increase FEAR and anxiety 22nd July 2013 https://www.sciencedaily.com/releases/2013/07/130722123206.htm

8. Adrenal Fatigue Medical News Today Is adrenal fatigue a real condition?https://www.medicalnewstoday.com/articles/245810.php

9. The Guardian Sally Challen walks free as court rules out retrial for killing abusive husband 7th June 2019 https://www.theguardian.com/uk-news/2019/jun/07/sally-challen-will-not-face-retrial-for-killing-husband

10. Justice for Women Sally Challen Appeal https://www.justiceforwomen.org.uk/sally-challen-appeal

11. The Telegraph Could Sally Challen's lawyer change history today? 27th February 2019 https://www.telegraph.co.uk/women/life/could-sally-challens-lawyer-change-history-today/

12. Woman's Aid What is Coercive Control https://www.womensaid.org.uk/information-support/what-is-domestic-abuse/coercive-control/

13. Gaslight 1938 play by Patrick Hamilton https://en.wikipedia.org/wiki/Gas_Light

14. Pete Walker Complex PTSD: From Surviving to Thriving: A GUIDE AND MAP FOR RECOVERING FROM CHILDHOOD TRAUM Publisher: CreateSpace Independent Publishing Platform; 1st ed edition (13 Dec. 2013) ISBN-10: 1492871842 ISBN-13: 978-1492871842

15. DEMENTOR'S KISS The Harry Potter Lexicon Dementors https://www.hp-lexicon.org/creature/dark-creatures/dementors/

16. ECHO Wikipedia Echo (mythology) https://en.wikipedia.org/wiki/Echo_(mythology)

17. Dr Craig Malkin The Spectrum: From Echoism to Narcissistic Personality Disorder http://www.drcraigmalkin.com/blog/narcissistic-personality-disorder

18. A Conscious Rethink What Flying Monkeys Do For Narcissists (And How To Disarm Them) https://www.aconsciousrethink.com/6891/avoid-flying-monkeys/

19. FLYING MONKEYS The Wonderful Wizard of Oz written by L. Frank Baum originally published by the George M. Hill Company May 17, 1900.

20. Healthy Narcissism Narcissisms Child What Is Healthy Narcissism? 14th May 2015 http://narcissismschild.com/2015/05/14/what-is-healthy-narcissism/

21. Jackson Mackenzie Psychopath Free (expanded edition) Publisher: BERKLEY - US; Expanded ed. edition (3 Sept. 2015) ISBN-10: 9780425279991 ISBN-13: 978-0425279991

22. Narcissistic Fleas Kim Saeed https://kimsaeed.com/2014/03/02/the-shocking-truth-staying-with-a-narcissist-may-give-you-fleas/

23. Red Flags The Railway Children E Nesbit various publishers Available free on line https://en.wikisource.org/wiki/The_Railway_Children/Chapter_6

24. Scapegoat https://en.wikipedia.org/wiki/Scapegoating

25. Metropolitan Police What is Rape and Sexual Assault https://www.met.police.uk/advice/advice-and-information/rsa/rape-and-sexual-assault/what-is-rape-and-sexual-assault/

26. S is for Stockholm Syndrome https://en.wikipedia.org/wiki/Stockholm_syndrome

27. Dr Patrick Carnes Phd The Betrayal Bond: Breaking Free of Exploitative Relationships Publisher: Health Communications (30 April 1998) ISBN-10: 1558745262 ISBN-13: 978-1558745261

28. Eckhart Tolle article Eckhart on the Dark Night of the soulhttps://www.eckharttolle.com/eckhart-on-the-dark-night-of-the-soul/

29. Ho'oponopono https://www.reviveyoursoul.co.uk/single-post/2015/09/16/Ho%E2%80%99oponopono

30. Befriending your PPF Stephen Palmer and Christine Wilding Beat Low Self-Esteem With CBT 1. Introducing Your Personal Fault Finder Publisher: Teach Yourself (26 Mar. 2010 ISBN-10: 0340991518 ISBN-13: 978-0340991510

31. Top 100 traits & behaviours of Personality-Disordered Individuals https://outofthefog.website/traits

32. https://www.reviveyoursoul.co.uk/single-post/2020/01/07/The-Dark-Night-of-the-Soul

YouTube

Thriver TV Melanie Tonia Evans
https://www.melanietoniaevans.com/

Knowing the Narcissist H.G .Tudor
https://narcsite.com/

Inner Integration Meredith Miller
https://www.innerintegration.com/

Spartan Life Coach Richard Grannon
http://spartanlifecoach.com/

A Journey Thru Wellness Johanna Kujath
http://journeythruwellness.com/

Kim Saeed
https://kimsaeed.com/

Quote References

A • Glennon Doyle momastery.com Blog Pain is not a mistake 21st April 2015 https://momastery.com/blog/2015/04/21/pain-mistake/

B • Gautama Buddha goodreads.com https://www.goodreads.com/quotes/3181192-in-the-end-only-three-things-matter-how-much-you

C • AA Milne Winnie the Pooh Library goodreads.com https://www.goodreads.com/quotes/6659295-you-are-braver-than-you-believe-stronger-than-you-seem

D • Brene Brown brainyquote.com https://www.brainyquote.com/quotes/brene_brown_553072

E • Joan of Arc goodreads.com https://www.goodreads.com/quotes/84842-one-life-is-all-we-have-and-we-live-it

F • Mother Teresa brainyquote.com https://www.brainyquote.com/quotes/mother_teresa_130839

G • Anne Frank brainyquote.com https://www.brainyquote.com/quotes/anne_frank_121584

H • Dolly Parton brainyquote.com https://www.brainyquote.com/quotes/dolly_parton_635063

I • Carl Jung brainyquote.com https://www.brainyquote.com/quotes/carl_jung_146686

J • Eleanor Roosevelt, You Learn by Living: Eleven Keys for a More Fulfilling Life goodreads.com https://www.goodreads.

com/quotes/3823-you-gain-strength-courage-and-confidence-by-every-experience-in

K • Gabor Mate interview with Tim Ferris YouTube https://youtu.be/H9B5mYfBPlY

L • Maya Angelou goodreads.com https://www.goodreads.com/quotes/11877-my-mission-in-life-is-not-merely-to-survive-but

M • Meredith Grey The Minds Journal https://themindsjournal.com/20-greys-anatomy-quotes-really-make-think/

N • Rosa Parks brainy quote.com https://www.brainyquote.com/quotes/rosa_parks_743670

O • Mark Anthony Ambition Quote http://www.quoteambition.com/best-strong-women-quotes-images/

P • Rumi brainyquote.com https://www.brainyquote.com/quotes/rumi_597890

Q • Washington Irving brainy quote.com https://www.brainyquote.com/quotes/washington_irving_149294

R • Audrey Hepburn brainy quote.com https://www.brainyquote.com/quotes/audrey_hepburn_126745

S • Eckhart Tolle brainyquote.com https://www.brainyquote.com/quotes/eckhart_tolle_571595

T • Buddha brainyquote.com https://www.brainyquote.com/quotes/buddha_104025

U • Rumi goodreads.com https://www.goodreads.com/quotes/103315-the-wound-is-the-place-where-the-light-enters-you

V • Confucius brainyquote.com https://www.brainyquote.com/quotes/confucius_101164

W • Nikola Tesla brainyquote.com https://www.brainyquote.com/quotes/nikola_tesla_596909

X • Mark Twain brainyquote.com https://www.brainyquote.com/quotes/mark_twain_133066

Y • Oscar Wilde brainyquote.com https://www.brainyquote.com/quotes/oscar_wilde_105222

Z • Marilyn Monroe goodreads.com https://www.goodreads.com/quotes/12379-i-believe-that-everything-happens-for-a-reason-people-change

Lightning Source UK Ltd.
Milton Keynes UK
UKHW022158021220
374515UK00011BA/2732

9 781916 357709